What others are
Make My Mar

"*Your mindset determines your results. This book will increase your marketing mindset, guaranteed!*"
    ~ **T. Harv Eker**, #1 NY Times Bestselling Author of *Secrets of the Millionaire Mind*

"*If you want to ROCK your marketing here's my suggestion: READ this book, IMPLEMENT what you learn & see the RESULTS in your business!*"
    ~ **Christine Comaford**, NY Times Bestselling Author of *Rules For Renegades*

"<u>*Make My Marketing Work*</u> *isn't just a great read; it's a take-you-by-the-hand blueprint that unlocks the mysteries used by ALL mega-successful marketers. These are the exact same tactics used by the best of the best, and now they are available for anyone with the desire to take charge of their destiny and stop making excuses.*"
    ~ "*Million Dollar*" **Mike Morgan**, Copywriter responsible for $250,000,000+ in sales

"*Finally, a marketing book that combines a philosophical point of view with practical guidelines for taking action, getting results and measuring your progress. No pie-in-the-sky empty promises, this a great read with immediately applicable advice that works. I couldn't operate my business without this book!*"
    ~**Libby Gill**, Executive Coach, Brand Strategist, and Bestselling Author of "*You Unstuck*"

"Marketing is a huge part of my company and the brand I am a part of. _Make My Marketing Work_ is an easy read with great thoughts and processes to help any business or brand improve. I recommend that anybody in charge of helping their company or brand grow to read this book and more importantly put what you learn into action."
~ **Jay Montgomery**, Owner 1-800-GOT-JUNK? Denver

"There are very few books as practical as this! Whether you're starting a new business or looking to grow an existing business you need to read this book. _Make My Marketing Work_ has created a tool that is destined to become the quintessential workbook for entrepreneurial success. Not since the E-myth have I read a book this useful."
~ **Mark McColman**, President, Kintec Footlabs Inc.

"_Make My Marketing Work_ is one of the best real world, practical manuals for marketing I have ever come across. It gives exceptional ideas on every page but also goes one step further than most by providing additional exercises and tips that allow you to develop your marketing as you go. This is a book that can actually help you dramatically improve your marketing and therefore improve your sales and profits! This is a book I am going to recommend to every client and entrepreneur I know."
~ **Martin H. Park**, President, Evolve Business Group Inc.

"Make My Marketing Work has done for marketing what the GPS has done for road navigation. An essential business marketing tool to help you select your destination and find the best way to navigate there.

Follow the experienced direction provided in Make My Marketing Work and you'll certainly choose the best way to optimize your business success through your marketing efforts."

~ **Gary Kemper**, General Manager, Consortium

"Easy to read, easy to understand, easy to implement! Make My Marketing Work is an essential book to add to your arsenal of business growth tools."

~ **Andrew Latchford**, COO, Cactus Club Resturants

"Make My Marketing Work is a great step-by-step guide to Marketing Mastery!"

~ **Robert Kenfield**, Founder, DreamLife Design

"FANTASTIC! An easy to read yet insightful book packed full of awesome tools to help dramatically grow revenues in your business."

~ **Michelle Fish**, Founder & CEO Integra Staffing; Bankston Partners; and The Diversity Forum

"An essential read for any small business owner!"

~ **Dean Gagnon**, President, CityMax.com

"In today's tough economic climate you need all the help you can get. This book not only gives you the tools, but also the know-how to successfully implement them into your business."

~ **Rahim Talib**, CEO, Meadow Fresh Dairy Products

"This book has become our marketing plan. As a small business we have been looking for a marketing strategy that will touch a variety of avenues. In this book we have found a step-by-step plan, which will allow us the ability to gage our future marketing efforts. For our small business this has become our marketing handbook."

~ **David Litherland**, Managing Partner-Vancouver Summit Search Group

"Having built a $1.7bn company and been named as a Top 20 CEO in BC, I know the importance of a strong strategic marketing platform. Make My Marketing Work is an amazing and easy to understand tool for any business owner looking to make those first important steps towards building an amazing company and brand!"

~ **David E Coe**, Former CEO DairyLand

"Strong marketing and a dynamic passion for people and culture is at the very core of our brand at McNeill Nakamoto Recruitment Group. This book really helps to capture all the elements that have made us successful and gives the reader an easy to understand road map to follow towards success!"

~ **Cheryl Nakamoto**, Chief, People Progress Potential, McNeill Nakamoto Recruitment Group

"WOW—finally a book that's as easy to implement as it is to read! Unlike "story" books where you have to search for the hidden meaning, Make My Marketing Work really hits home exactly what you need to do and how you need to do it!"

~ **Brad Carpenter**, CEO Solus Decor Inc

"_Make My Marketing Work_ provides concrete solutions for businesses of all sizes. The principles addressed in the book are comprehensive and complete yet easy to implement. _Make My Marketing Work_ is a must read for entrepreneurs and management at all levels of any enterprise."
 ~ **Jeff Duncan**, Founder & COO Meetingmax.cc

"Business is fiercely competitive. The customization of any business offering is heavily reliant on strategic, customized marketing, both online and offline. _Make My Marketing Work_ is a fantastic business resource full of innovative marketing concepts, ideas, examples and actions. Do the exercises! You'll finish a great read and create a customized marketing action plan for your business."
 ~ **Minto Roy**, President/Partner Careers Today Canada/ Snaptech Marketing Group

"Paul and Alex know marketing. I had the privilege of working directly with these guys and saw first hand the magic they bring to marketing. Anyone in business will benefit from the simple marketing magic shared here."
 ~ **Ken Johnston**, CEO HeartSound Consulting

make
MY MARKETING
work

How to Win Customers
& Make More Money

paul KEETCH
alex READ

New York

Make My Marketing Work
How to Win Customers & Make More Money

ISBN 978-1-60037-753-2

Library of Congress Control Number: 2010921181

Morgan James Publishing
1225 Franklin Ave., STE 325
Garden City, NY 11530-1693
Toll Free 800-485-4943
www.MorganJamesPublishing.com

Acknowledgments

This book could not have been written without the help of a talented team of professionals whose time and dedication supported its creation.

Specifically, our gratitude goes to Jonathan Galbraith (www.BaseTwoMedia.com) for his help with audio production; Sandy Gerber & Karley Cunningham (www.3DegreesWest.ca) for their expertise in web development & design; Matt Samycia Wood (www.SamyciaWood.com) for his design and branding expertise; and Ron Edgar (www.SalesPitBull.com) for his valuable insight into the marriage of marketing & sales.

And of course, to our families for their unwavering support and the countless thousands of business owners around the world whose experiences trying to build a successful business inspired us to write this book—may it serve you well.

Contents

Foreword From The Authors

Don't consider this just "another marketing book"—it is much more than that.

Typically, marketing books focus on specific marketing tactics that you can use to grow your business. Unfortunately, there is often no prerequisite offered to let you know whether or not you need ~ and can actually profit from ~ any one particular tactic.

The books that do cover marketing strategy either go into so much depth as to require that you already have a marketing degree... or they gloss over core concepts, assuming you already understand them.

We strove to ensure that Make My Marketing Work would fill those gaps and do exactly as the title suggests: make your marketing work to grow your business strategically over the long term so that you get exactly what you want out of it.

Consider this book (and the online resources that accompany it) a sophisticated GPS device for your business. You already know where you are right now and you've probably got a pretty good idea of where you want to go. (If not, we'll cover that first, so don't worry about it if your future goals are not clear to you yet—they will be soon enough.)

Once you know those two coordinates (the present and the future) simply input the information and use the exercises and resources we've compiled for you to outline the specific directions that will take your business from where you are to where you want to be.

1

There is one catch, however (there always is, isn't there?). In order to get to your intended destination, you're going to have to actually do the work.

That means creating an account at
www.MakeMyMarketingWorkBook.com
and downloading all of the tools, resources and worksheets you'll need to complete the exercises we've prepared for you.

It means sharpening your pencil, shutting the door and turning off your email while you read and work on your business.

It means creating your strategic marketing plan and then actually implementing the necessary tactics in real time, in the real world.

Just like a GPS device cannot actually start, accelerate and steer your car, so it is with this book. Reading it won't change a thing.

Doing the exercises and applying what you learn will.

It's a simple formula, really:
(Knowledge + Experience) * Action = Results

So download the resources at
www.MakeMyMarketingWorkBook.com, grab your pencil and a cup of coffee and let's get started …

Paul Keetch
Vancouver, Canada

So what are you going to learn in

Make My Marketing Work?

This book is broken into modules which take an in-depth and interactive look at the various elements of a successful marketing strategy.

 We'll begin by taking a look at the business you operate and the market to which you'll be promoting and culminate with your marketing funnel, so you gain a complete understanding of how to really make money from your efforts.

The processes are interactive and designed to raise the temperature on your "marketing thermostat" even if it's an area you think you know already!

Here's a glimpse of what's in store to get you prepared for the marketing journey you are about to undertake!

Section 1 :: Know My Business

Without a little introspection, how are you going to be able to create an **amazing** marketing strategy? In order to start creating your strategy you need to know everything that impacts your marketing efforts. This goes for everything from defining your company culture and brand to developing your product structure and lifecycle. Running full on in the wrong direction could prove costly. So we'll show you how to make sure all your stars are aligned ...

Section 2 :: My Market Intelligence

Before you launch anything, you need to have a firm understanding of the market you will be serving. What are the demographics; what is the economic climate; what has worked and what has failed? There are a ton of variables that can impact the effectiveness of your marketing. This is especially true when you consider who is out there trying to steal your lunch! How can you prepare for the competitive landscape on a global scale and still stay in budget? Your greatest competitor might not even be on your radar but we will show you how to be ready and adapt ...

Section 3 :: My Marketing Message

Which is more important - what you say or how you say it? It's a bit like asking if the chicken or the egg came first. One without the other just doesn't work very well, so we'll cover both. Finding your own voice in today's market can be tough, so we'll examine the different methods you can use. Once you've created that great message the only person who's heard it is you! You have to get the message **out there** to the right people at the right time if you're going to be successful.

This section will also discuss the different methods that are available to you to get your message out effectively. We'll look at everything from traditional advertising to viral campaigns. There are some amazing opportunities out there for you to get your message out cheaply and effectively. You might even come up with a few of your own ...

Section 4 :: Continue My Marketing

How will you know if everything you learn and apply in this book is really working to grow your business? We will teach you ways to accurately track your results so you can see what is working and where you need to improve.

Remember: the most basic premise of all is **"Do more** of what works and less of what doesn't".

We'll then show you how to create a marketing funnel and deployment strategy that will ensure you can effectively get your message across and turn it into revenue, the lifeblood of your business.

Section 5 :: Pulling It All Together

Finally, we're going to pull everything together. We'll look at the most critical aspect of understanding what to do with all the great new information you've learnt and ideas you've generated!

All this is geared towards helping you take **ACTION**. It will be this action that distinguishes whether you get good results from the book you're about to read vs. getting **great results!**

So ...

Like we said at the start, each section will be interactive and experience based. By the time you complete the book, you will have a great working knowledge of the concepts taught and what to do with them. You will have the opportunity to practice each skill as you learn how to.....

Make *YOUR* Marketing Work!

If you haven't already done so you should register your book at:

www.MakeMyMarketingWorkBook.com

Then, download all of the bonus forms and worksheets we've provided. You'll need them as you go through the book.

Alright, let's get on with the program...

SECTION 1 :: Know My Business

In This Section You Will:

✓ Develop your marketing vision.
✓ Learn the true essence of branding and how your internal company culture affects your overall customer experience.
✓ Understand the importance of modeling and identify at least one organization you wish to model in your own business.
✓ Discover the "4 Ps" of marketing and how they fit into each stage of the product lifecycle.
✓ Be introduced to the product adoption cycle.

Develop My Marketing Vision

We're assuming you already have some kind of vision for your company.

It might be to be the biggest, the best or the brightest in your industry. It might be to deliver a certain experience or level of service to your customers. It might be to generate $x by a certain date.

Whatever it is doesn't really matter, as long as it is something. You can't hit a target unless you know what it is that you're aiming for!

And just as your business needs an overall vision, your marketing must have a vision that supports it.

You might want to:

• Generate more leads

- Convert more leads to clients
- Develop new markets or attract new market segments
- Increase the average value per sale
- Remarket new products to your existing clients in order to increase your LCV (lifetime customer value)

As you can see, there are many things you can focus on and those are just the tip of the iceberg. By creating a basic understanding of your marketing vision, we can then create the "focus" and "alignment" needed to successfully implement the remainder of the program.

◀)) Insider Tip:

In order for your marketing to be truly effective, it must have focus. In order to get focus, you must know where you're going. Your vision creates the potential for it becoming real. That's why we get you to write down your goals and visualize the outcome before we even think about getting into the data! **As Vincent Van Gogh said, "I dream my painting and paint my dream."** You must do the same thing by creating a marketing vision and then acting upon that vision to make it a reality. Visualize it first, then make it a reality!

Your marketing vision must reflect the overall vision of the company or it will not resonate with you, your team or your customers. So if your company vision is to reach one million new prospects in the next five years, but your marketing vision is to remarket only to existing clients then your two visions are out of alignment and conflict with each other.

 **Exercise:**

Create Your Marketing Vision!

Pull out your overall business vision for reference and have it close to hand. Now, grab some paper (or a big dry-erase board) and start to brainstorm the elements of what your marketing vision might be. You can be SMART (specific, measurable, actionable, realistic, time phased) if you want to, but for brainstorming the creativity should be off the charts! Write as much as you can about what you want to achieve from your marketing efforts—just make sure it aligns with your company goals and vision. We'll come back to this brainstorm later and refine it in greater depth.

Download the Business Vision worksheet at www.MakeMyMarketingWorkBook.com.

Branding, Culture and the Customer Experience

Having a powerful brand is not something you can get just by answering a few questions and creating a sexy logo. Yes, you need to have the **OOH, AAH** factor, but it is the effort made over the long term to provide a continuity of experience with each and every interaction that truly builds your brand.

Your brand (including company culture) is an integral part of your marketing efforts, and in the end nothing is cooler, sexier or packs more wow than a repeat customer who loves what your brand delivers!

When first looking at creating a marketing plan to develop a brand, many business owners get confused by thinking that their logo *is* their brand. We know YOU would never think that, but it's worth repeating ... loudly.

YOUR LOGO IS NOT YOUR BRAND!

Now you say it:
My logo is NOT my brand!

Once more, twice as loud:
MY LOGO IS NOT MY BRAND!

Okay, now that we've got that out of our system, let's look at what branding really is and how it applies to your marketing efforts.

First and foremost, as we've discussed, your brand is not your logo (sorry, couldn't). It is also not the product you sell, your website, tradeshow booth or marketing materials. Although these things are all elements of what make up your brand, they are distinctly not your brand.

Your brand is the promise you make, whether specified or implied, and—pay attention because this is the important part—*how you deliver on that promise in the minds of your customers and prospects.*

Said differently, your brand is a collection of the perceptions of your company in the minds of your customers. Your "customers" are more than just the people who buy from you. In fact, you have three distinctly different groups of "customers" and the touch points, or ways you interact with them, vary by each group.

Your 3 Customer Types:
1. The people who buy (or are looking to buy) what you're selling.
2. Your vendors and suppliers.
3. Your employees.

Your customers are both external and internal. They are of equal importance to your brand, your company and your success.

Let's look at each group in a little more detail.

Customer #1 – People Who Buy From You

People who buy from you are the ones who pay you for your products or services and represent the traditional concept of a customer.

The touch points you have with this customer, or how they interact with your company, is a large and very, very important list.

This list includes:
- Your marketing copy (wording) on:
    - Your flyers
    - Your brochures
    - Your business cards
    - Your advertising
- Your website (look, feel, usability, copy / content)

- Your tradeshow booth
- Your storefront
- Your sales force
- Your customer service team
- Your shipping warehouse
- Your finance department (like when you have to process a refund)
- Your receptionist or automated voice system customers get when they call your business
- Your cleanliness (hey you reflect your business, right!)
- Your reputation
- Your logo and all the ways you use it
- And much, much more!

 # Exercise:

Write down at least 5 more touch points that you think affect the perceptions of the people who purchase from you.

Download the Customer Touch Points worksheet at www.MakeMyMarketingWorkBook.com.

Customer Type #2 – Your Vendors and Suppliers

The people you do business with on a business-to-business level are also your customers and how you work with them also affects your overall perception in the marketplace. Since the collective perception is your overall brand value, the companies you do business with are a big element of your brand.

Some of the touch points for your vendors and suppliers are:
- Your shipping & receiving department
- Accounts payable
- Purchasing department

 Exercise:

Identify and write down 3 more ways that you think your vendors and suppliers interact with your company.

Download the Customer Touch Points worksheet at www.MakeMyMarketingWorkBook.com.

Customer #3 – Your Employees

Have you ever considered your staff members to be customers of your company? If not, it's time you started because their opinion is possibly the most important one of them all.

Why?

Simple - your staff are the ones who interact with your customers every single day. They create the experience that your external customers have—both the ones who buy what you're selling and the vendors who help you do it.

Just some of the myriad touch points that your employees experience week in and week out at your company:
- Initial interview
- Availability of parking

- Internal rewards and incentive programs
- Remuneration (salary & bonuses)
- Benefits
- The type of toilet paper in the washrooms (if you think we're kidding then you probably should ask your staff what they think about that!)
- And there are literally hundreds of other examples...

 Exercise:

In a note book, add at least 5 more touch points that affect your staff. Put yourself in their shoes and think back to a time when you were the employee rather than the employer.

Download the Customer Touch Points worksheet at www.MakeMyMarketingWorkBook.com.

Creating Culture

Culture, just like your brand, is a reflection of you and your values. Your staff takes direction from you. What you say and do is important—as is how you say and do it!

In fact, the "how" is much more important because it is the example you set, rather than the rules you make that will ultimately influence behavior.

🔊)) Insider Tip:

Monkey See, Monkey Do!

Modeling is one of the most powerful forms of influence that you have at your disposal. Use it wisely and you will get a powerful workforce who represents your company the way you would, and who are fiercely loyal to you.

But if you get it wrong by setting a bad example or by not aligning the example you set with your own rules for conduct, your employees are going to notice.

They may not say anything, at least not at first, but they will notice. Pretty soon your customers are going to notice as well. Try as you might, your service levels will go down, refund requests will go up and staff turnover will go through the roof.

Just like your customers, most employees won't let you know directly how they're feeling. Instead, they will take their business (in this case, their skills and abilities) somewhere else. You won't know anything was wrong until they're already gone and by then it's way too late to do anything about it.

Gandhi said, *"Be the change you wish to see in the world."*

At Make My Marketing Work, we say:
"Monkey see, monkey do."

It has been said that imitation is the best form of flattery. But if you are modeling behavior that is contrary to what you want your employees to do, this "flattery" is going to be counter-productive.

Now, exactly how you want to create your culture is up to you to decide. It all depends on your core values and what is truly important to you.

Some things are easy to do and others are harder. Some things don't cost you anything and other things can cost lots of money. But one thing is sure, no matter what you do: **your company will have a culture**.

The only question then is: will you proactively create your culture (and your brand) or will you let it happen "willy nilly"?

Here are some things you can do to ensure that you create the kind of culture that is important to you:

1. **Remember your own pet peeves**—Think back to your days as an employee and try to remember the things you griped about.

2. **Involve your staff in strategic processes**—Even if you don't always use their ideas, letting them contribute to the process will allow them to know they were heard, understand the process and buy in to the final decision.

3. **Reward top performers**—Regularly (and publicly) acknowledging and rewarding the top performers will inspire similar behavior in others. Just be sure that the performance levels required to be

rewarded are fully disclosed so that no one has to guess what they need to do.

4. **Fire poor performers**—There is almost nothing that will de-motivate your staff faster than allowing lazy or unqualified employees to stick around. Everyone makes a bad hire now and again. You'll be doing everyone a favor by weeding out the bad seeds.

5. **Create a mentoring culture**—Provide opportunities for your employees to grow not only in their position and within the organization, but as individuals as well.

6. **Profit sharing**—A tough pill for many private business owners to swallow, but if you develop a profit-sharing program where your staff is directly benefiting from the success of the company, they will be much more likely to do whatever it takes for everyone to be successful.

7. **Put the right people in the right job**—You need some super high performers in certain positions (sales, marketing and customer service, etc) but you also need some people who are more than thrilled to do mundane work such as filing, admin tasks, etc. Get the right people in the right role and everyone will be happy.

8. **Offer "well days" in addition to "sick days"**— Helping your employees with their work/life balance will make them more productive in the long run. Create a "well day" program where employees can call in "well" so that they can go do something they are passionate about.

 **Exercise:**

Identify the top 5 values that are important to you personally in proactively creating your company culture. Then identify at least 5 things you can implement to enhance one or more of those values in your workplace this month!

Download the Values worksheet at www.MakeMyMarketingWorkBook.com.

Pick A Model ... Any Model

Modeling is an important and powerful way to increase the power of your culture and brand.

Is customer service one of your top priorities? If so, check out how companies like West Jet, Jet Blue, Enterprise Rent-A-Car, Ritz Carlton Hotels or Petsmart all manage their customer service process.

Or maybe you really want to build a company based on having a cool internal culture? Then you'd best look at Google, Starbucks, Yahoo!,

1-800-GOT-JUNK? or Back in Motion Rehab.

Simply find companies that are already doing what you want to do, look at what they do, and then model this behavior.

 ## Exercise:

List the number one value that is important to you and identify some companies that model that value. Then look at what they are doing and how they are doing it.

The Marketing Mix—The 4 Ps of Marketing

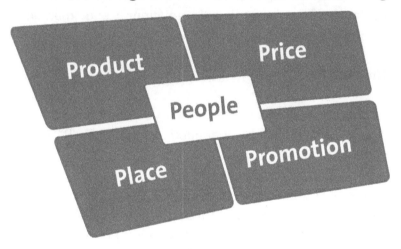

The marketing mix consists of four primary elements:

Product – The tangible product or service features. This includes such things as: brand name, functionality, design, styling, quality, safety, packaging design, repairs, support and warranty.

Price – The price your customer will pay for the product or service, including: pricing strategy, manufacturer's suggested retail price (MSRP), volume discounts, wholesale pricing, bundling and seasonal pricing. Price also includes the perceived value of your service.

Place – The location where the product or service is available for purchase: distribution channels, market coverage (exclusivity, selective distribution, etc), warehousing, inventory management and order processing.

Promotion – All aspects of communication as it relates to your product or service. We'll cover this in much more detail throughout this book, including: promotional strategy; advertising; public relations; and marketing communications.

The Fifth P?

Of course, all of this is irrelevant if you don't have a target market, which can be identified as the fifth "P" in the marketing mix—people!

People – The primary and secondary target audiences for your product or service. These groups include: existing customers; customers of the competition; people who are actively searching for your product or service; and people who don't yet know they have a need, but one day will.

The final "mix" (how each element fits together) of each will be different depending on your specific business and where your product sits in the product lifecycle, but all four elements should be taken into account when planning your overall marketing strategy.

 **Exercise:**

Define the basic 4 "Ps" for each product or service that your business offers (we'll cover the fifth "P" very soon).

Download the Marketing Mix worksheet at www.MakeMyMarketingWorkBook.com.

The Product Lifecycle

The marketing mix described above will be different depending on your unique situation and there are several factors that affect the specific mix you will use given your current place in the product lifecycle.

The product lifecycle generally flows in five stages of growth and decline, beginning when you **first introduce** it and ending when you eventually take it off the market.

Even seemingly indestructible companies like Coca Cola will eventually have to take their products off the market as profitability declines to the point where it is not feasible to continue. In many cases, strong brands like Coke can adapt their product to meet new consumer trends (such as awareness of health concerns, etc) and modify the original product in order to **reinvigorate it** and spark consumer interest again.

Cherry Coke, Diet Coke, Vanilla Coke, Caffeine Free Coke, are all examples of the lifecycle of the Coca Cola brand.

The five stages of product lifecycle are:
1. Development
2. Introduction
3. Growth
4. Maturity
5. Decline

1) Development

In the development stage, you are doing market research and product development to ensure that the product or service is viable in the market place. For the purpose of this book, we will assume that you already have a product or service developed that you intend to market.

2) Introduction

During the introduction process, sales will likely be slow as consumers become aware of your product and the benefits it can provide them. The goal during this phase is to reaffirm your initial concept validation by establishing a base market and building demand.

In this phase, your advertising costs are likely to be quite high as you work to establish your product in the minds of the consumers. You will be specifically targeting the "innovators" and "early adopters" (two groups of people who typically use or "adopt" new products and services early in their lifecycle).

The more creative you can be to gain exposure for your company the better. Think way outside the box, but keep within your brand integrity.

Marketing Mix in the Introduction Phase:
• **Product** – Focus on one or two core benefits only.

- **Price** – Generally high in order to recoup initial investment quickly, however; lower penetration pricing strategies may be employed to gain market share quickly.
- **Place** – Often selective and somewhat scattered as you begin to implement your distribution plan and see what works and what doesn't.
- **Promotion** – Primarily aimed at building product and brand awareness, samples or free trials may be employed and directed towards innovators and early adopters.

3) Growth—Spread the Word!

This phase commences when the product or service has gained a foothold in the marketplace and the innovators and early adopters are actively talking about you and your product. Ideally, this phase involves rapid revenue growth and expansion of distribution methods as distributors actively seek you out.

Word of mouth and referral marketing are leveraged during the growth phase. Advertising costs can also generally be seen to increase as well as generate a **higher return** on investment than in the introduction phase. Early adopters and the early majority are now aware of your product and are purchasing from you, while the interest levels of the late majority are rising.

The primary goal during the growth phase is to establish yourself as the leader in your given market. During this time you should also begin looking outward to new markets and market segments that can be exploited.

Marketing Mix in the Growth Phase:
- **Product** – Expand product features and benefits, improve product quality.
- **Price** – Maintain the price at a high level if sales remain strong or reduce to leverage growth and capture additional market share.
- **Place** – New distribution methods are actively sought and implemented.
- **Promotion** – Advertising is increased to create greater brand awareness and generally returns higher ROI. Word of mouth and referral programs are increased to leverage positive positioning.

4) Maturity—Let it Ride!

This stage is generally the most profitable since volume should result in lower overall costs and advertising can be reduced since brand awareness is now very strong. In this phase, sales **continue to grow** although likely at a slower rate than previously as competitors enter the market. An increase in competition may result in decreased market share and a lowering of prices.

The early majority of consumers continue to buy through this phase and the late majority joins the mix as well.

Marketing efforts are aimed at getting customers to switch brands and increasing usage of existing customers. The primary goal during this phase is to maintain market share and extend the product lifecycle by extending into new markets or market segments, which can spur a revitalization of the growth phase.

Marketing Mix in the Maturity Phase:
- **Product** – Modifications may be needed to differentiate yourself from the rise in competitors with a similar offering.
- **Price** – It may be necessary to reduce prices in order to maintain market share.
- **Place** – Incentives to resellers in order to maintain shelf space and visibility over your competition and new distribution channels are sought.
- **Promotion** – Brand loyalty is highlighted here, as well as enticing customers away from the competition with special promotions and incentives.

5) Decline—What goes up ...
Eventually, sales are going to begin to decline as the marketplace becomes saturated with competitors or when your technology or product becomes obsolete. Customer tastes may also change causing sales to decline.

In the decline phase you can elect to discontinue a product line and sell off your existing inventory, coast through the decline trying to get as much profit as possible before discontinuing the line or you can maintain the product hoping that competition will exit the market before you, resulting in an increase in market share.

Sales in this phase come primarily from the laggards as well as from some of the late majority who may not yet have purchased.

You may elect to **revamp** and **re-release** the product with new features or technologies that are adapted to the current marketplace. Doing so can provide a new means of differentiation and can revitalize your sales.

Marketing Mix in the Decline Phase:
- **Product** – The number of products may be reduced and certain products may be revamped in order to make them look new.
- **Price** – Prices may be lowered to liquidate inventory of products that are going to be discontinued or maintained for products that are being rejuvenated.
- **Place** – Distribution channels that are no longer profitable are phased out and eliminated and niche channels are sought to selectively reach a smaller segment of buyers.
- **Promotion** – Advertising is dramatically reduced or eliminated in order to maintain margins with lowered prices. Efforts continue to be aimed at supporting the brand for any continued products or services and getting the laggards to buy.

Okay, so now you know all about the product lifecycle and can use this knowledge to make decisions on how you implement the marketing mix during each phase. But ...

Yes, there is a "but" ...

This is not an exact science and we would hate for you to cut your advertising spending just because sales declined in one quarter and you thought that declining sales meant that you were in the decline phase.

A decrease in sales could be caused by a slight economic shift in the local market, by a rise in gas prices or a labor strike and could easily self-correct or be corrected with the right course of action. Or it could be time to hang up this particular product and move on ... as Robert Frost said, "Be sure to sell your horse before its dead".

The Product Adoption Cycle

One last thing we want to share with you in this section is the different ways or approach that customers take to market. You can expect to come across all of them in your business. We call them "Customer Personalities".

It is important to know so that you can target your marketing communications appropriately, depending on where you are in the product diffusion curve.

There are five types of customer personalities and each behaves differently when making buying decisions.

1) Innovators – Well-informed risk takers who are willing to try out an unproven product.

2) Early Adopters – Based on the positive response of the innovators, early adopters (who tend to be educated opinion leaders) begin to purchase.

3) Early Majority – These are careful consumers who tend to avoid risk. This group will purchase once the product has been proven by the early adopters since they rely on the recommendations of others who have experience with a given product or service.

4) Late Majority – A somewhat skeptical group of consumers who only purchase after it has become commonplace.

5) Laggards – They avoid change at all cost and will only purchase when traditional alternatives are no longer available.

Time to review all your great ideas!

Go back and read your notes on developing a marketing vision and re-write any words or phrases that jump out. Think about your overall company vision and all the items we discussed in this section about branding, culture, modeling, etc.

Now bring all of that together and create your first draft marketing vision using the worksheet at www.MakeMyMarketingWorkBook.com. Remember, at the moment this is just the "what". After completing the program you'll also have the "how".

Once you have your final marketing vision (at the end of the program), write it out! Then take your marketing vision and print it out …

REALLY

BIG!

Once printed out, post it somewhere visible, where you and everyone else can see it every day. Talking about it to other people on a regular basis will continue to anchor it for you so that it becomes second nature.

Every time you need to make a marketing decision, look at your vision. Read it out loud. Ask yourself and your team if the decision you are considering is in line with your vision.

When the action you are about to take doesn't fit your vision then you are not aligned and your marketing message will reflect that misalignment. When you can say "Yes!" when you compare your marketing efforts against your vision to see if they are aligned, you know you're on the right track.

TIME OUT!
(Pause, Breath, Review)

You now have a basic **vision** of how your marketing will support your overall business vision and understand how your brand is affected by everything you do, including your internal culture.

You've also got someone to **model** who has already been where you are now and done what you aspire to do—remember to use this resource so you don't have to reinvent the wheel every time!

And you've learned what the four elements of the marketing mix are, how they fit into the product lifecycle and what the different types of consumers are.

Give yourself a small reward for completing the first section of this book—you deserve it!

SECTION 2 :: My Market Intelligence

In This Section You Will:

✓ Understand who and what your customers are.
✓ Discover what your Primary Target Market is.
✓ Discover what your Secondary Target Market is.
✓ Define and understand your competition.
✓ Know the importance of both direct and indirect competition.
✓ Become aware of your price and place in the market.

Know My Customers

Whether you already have an established business or are just getting started as an entrepreneur, knowing and understanding your target audience is of vital importance.

Getting this right will make running your business FUN as well as profitable. Get it wrong and you'll struggle needlessly.

Think about a time when you were looking to make a purchase, whether a small low-cost item such as dinner at a local restaurant or a large purchase like a new car or home. You probably had certain businesses that you preferred to deal with and certain businesses that you prefer not to deal with at all.

Maybe it is due to a customer service experience (positive or negative) you had in the past, the opinion of a trusted advisor, or possibly it was simply the way the store was designed or the product or brand they offered.

It's even possible that you just got a "bad feeling" somewhere along the way and that turned you off doing business with them forever.

Knowing your customer and market will help you understand the factors that affect those buying decisions.

Success in marketing relies almost entirely on building a trusting, personal connection with each one of your prospects. They must feel as though you are speaking to them directly with each and every interaction, even if you are speaking to many people at once as with mass media advertising.

To do this effectively, you must understand and empathize with who your customers and prospects are. You must know their **wants, needs and fears,** and be able to persuade them that your product or service is the perfect solution for their unique situation.

When you build relationships with your clients by meeting their needs (instead of your own) and by being a valuable resource for them, they are much more likely to give you their business, as well as refer additional business to you.

Forgetting or neglecting to be of service to them will have the exact opposite effect. Not only will they make an alternate buying decision or cease doing business with you, they will let all of their friends—and a few of their enemies—know that you are not a business to be trusted.

In order to *make your marketing work* over the long term, you must consciously develop and implement a plan to get to know your customers and potential customers on an intimate level.

In this section, you will gain the necessary knowledge and insight you'll need to do this, but knowledge alone is not enough.

What Are My Customers?

There are more than six billion people on planet earth that would all make suitable **target prospects** for your product or service.

Or are there?

More than likely, the answer is no. This is because certain **market segments** are more likely than others to consider purchasing your product.

Think about it for a second: if you manufacture women's shoes, does it make sense to spend 50% of your marketing budget trying to persuade men to purchase your shoes? Of course not—you would be wasting a good percentage of that money.

At the same time, it doesn't necessarily make sense to forget about men entirely when marketing your women's shoes either. After all, there are many reasons to buy shoes other than just style and comfort (we'll let you think about that one for a second). This is where *emotion* comes into play.

Understanding the **demographic profile** of your existing clients will help you make **strategic marketing decisions** that will have the greatest likelihood of generating the best return on investment (ROI) for your marketing efforts and dollars.

Your customer demographics include external characteristics like:

- Age
- Gender
- Ethnicity
- Geographic location
- Socio-economic status
- Religion
- Marital status
- Ownership (home, car, pet, etc.)
- Language(s) spoken
- Mobility
- Life cycles (fertility, mortality, migration)

 Exercise:

Write down 5 characteristics of your customer demographics.

Download the Customer Demographics worksheet at: www.MakeMyMarketingWorkBook.com.

Who Are My Customers?

"Each to their own taste," is how the old saying goes and whoever said it was talking about psychographics.

Psychographics are the **interests, attitudes and opinions** of your target market; what they like to do with their time and money, what they think about all manner of things and their prevailing attitudes, preconceptions and biases.

Using the earlier example of a women's shoe manufacturer, it's likely that the appropriate demographic for the high end shoe you're producing is a middle aged, middle to high income female, living in a densely populated area of North America. This is great information, but it doesn't tell the whole story.

If the stylish shoes you're producing or importing are made of high-grade genuine leather, and very expensive, it would obviously be a mistake to spend your marketing dollars in areas or neighborhoods that have a high concentration of low income earners who are mainly retired.

However, it would also be a mistake to specifically target members of animal rights groups as buyers of your leather shoes, no matter how much disposable income they may have! They already have a **pre-existing bias** against your product and whether you agree with them or not, you will waste your money trying to target this market segment.

◀)) Insider Tip:

Join The Conversation.
Each and every one of your prospective customers hasa conversation going on inside their own heads about what they fear & desire.

It's your job to enter the conversation that is already taking place instead of trying to force a brand new conversation, idea, thought or belief.

You need to understand and **meet the needs** of your customers. If you have a specific product that you want to market, then you need to find a distribution method that fits. If you have an area or distribution method you want to utilize, then you need to find a product that fits the area. It's a symbiotic relationship.

The personal interests, attitudes and opinions of people are what truly make them unique. Not only do you not want to spend precious marketing time, energy & dollars trying to **attract people** who already fit into a psychographic that conflicts with your product or service, you want to focus those same marketing dollars on customers that exactly match your target market.

 **Exercise:**

Write down 5 characteristics of your Customer Psychographics.

Download the Customer Psychographics worksheet at: www.MakeMyMarketingWorkBook.com.

Identifying My Primary Target Market

Your primary target market is comprised of people who are already looking for the solution you have to offer. They know they have a need and are actively searching for a solution. These are the **"low hanging fruit"** and are the easiest type of customer to focus on.

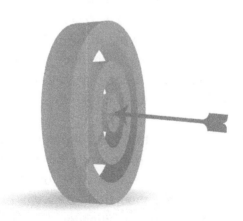

If you are currently in business, you can determine who your primary target market is by looking at your existing clients. Which of them would you consider to be your best customers? Who buys the most from you and naturally refers people to you because you are already so aligned with both what and who they are?

◀)) Insider Tip:

Remember the 80/20 rule.

80% of your dollars ($$) come from 20% of your customers. Figure out who they are, then work hard to find more customers just like them!

If you are just getting started in business, you will need to look to your competitors for insight into exactly who your primary target market is. Visit the store or website of people you consider to be your direct competition who are offering a product or service that is similar in nature to your own.

In either case, try talking directly to those people who are already buying what you have to sell. Ask them about **why they purchase** from you (or from your competitor) and what they look for when evaluating a product or service. Ask them about themselves - if they are married, where they live, their age group and their income bracket.

There are many ways to go about getting this information, but the easiest is to create a profile for each and every customer who does business with you. As you build the relationship and earn their trust, they will be increasingly willing to answer more questions about themselves, particularly if there is something in it for them. You can give them a discount or freebie in exchange for their information.

Identify My Secondary Target Market?

Eventually, you are going to need to look to your secondary target market in order to continue to **grow your business.** This is something that you might as well do during your initial research, even though you may not focus your efforts in this area for the first little while.

Your secondary markets are people who don't yet know that they require your product or service in order to solve a need. It's possible that they don't realize that they have a need, in which case you will have to work at making them aware that this is something they should be thinking about. Or you will have to work at **creating the desire** for your product or service, irrespective of whether they "need" it or not.

 Exercise:

Using the profiles of your customers, create a sample *Customer Profile* for your primary and secondary markets. These can be real or fictitious people that you will literally "speak to" when crafting your marketing message in later sections of this program.

Download the Customer Profile worksheet at: www.MakeMyMarketingWorkBook.com.

By identifying and understanding what and who your primary and secondary target markets are you will be able to communicate with your customers and prospects in a way that is most useful and effective for them. You can quickly

build rapport with anyone when you understand and relate to their primary fears and desires.

Knowing My Competition

Entering the marketplace ~ any marketplace ~ without knowing the competitive landscape would be like running into a dark room without knowing where the walls are. You may start off okay, but sooner or later you are going to run into something hard. Having **the right tools** in your belt (like a **competitive analysis**) can save you a lot of pain in the long run.

When you have a solid understanding of the competition you face, you will be better equipped to craft your essential message, unique selling proposition (USP) and customer "touch-points", all of which we will go into detail in this chapter. Plus, you will be able to identify and exploit opportunities as they develop within your marketplace before anyone else.

Being able to adapt to your competition will give a serious advantage to your business. When you have a **clear understanding** of what your competition does well (and doesn't do well) you can gear your marketing programs to put your business in a position of authority.

Knowledge of who your competition is will not only help you understand and evaluate what potential threats they may pose and what the major points of differentiation are between your company and theirs, it can also **spark your creativity** to come up with a unique solution to your customer's problem. Seeing how someone else is tackling a problem can lead to new insights that you may not have reached otherwise.

Defining The Competition

There is nothing worse than thinking you are completely prepared for something and then you get blind-sided and knocked off your feet. When defining your competition, look at it from all angles.

Look at:
- All of the factors that might draw your customers away from you.
- All of the factors that might draw their customers to you.
- What they have done in the past.
- What they are planning to do in the future.

Imagine for a moment that you are a restaurant owner serving a local delicacy. Who are your competitors?

 Of course, the other restaurants who also serve the same kind of delicacy are in competition with you. That's a **no brainer**. But, so are the restaurants who serve different kinds of food. What about fast food restaurants? You are all competing for the same entertainment dollars.

While you're at it, what about cinemas, live theatre and live music venues? And don't forget about cable television, DVD rentals and video game systems!

All of them could impact your revenue.

Think of this in 3 levels ...

1. **Direct** – Competitors who offer the same product or service (i.e. Mexican restaurant vs. Mexican restaurant)

2. **Indirect** – Businesses that compete for the same budget dollars (i.e. Mexican restaurant vs. Restaurants in general vs. DVD rentals, etc)

3. **Variable** – Businesses or economic conditions that could take revenue away or bring revenue in (i.e. Live theatre production or labor strike)

Can you see how all of these very different types of activities are all in competition with each other for a finite amount of money in a given marketplace? Having a restaurant is not just about serving food—it's also about providing an entertainment experience.

When considering who your competition is, remember to ask yourself what the experience is that your customers will ultimately have and what emotional need is being met. Then consider what their options are to get a similar experience.

 Exercise:

List 3 of your competitors or competitive factors at each of the 3 levels

Download the Competitor Analysis worksheet at: www.MakeMyMarketingWorkBook.com.

Becoming Aware of My Competitors

The quickest and easiest way to see how your product or service stands up against that of your competitors is to become a customer of theirs.

When you test your competition's ability to serve you as a client you will learn a lot more about their business than simply by visiting a website or retail store. You will **become clear** on what they do well in addition to the things they maybe don't do as well.

These will become your **points of differentiation.**

If possible, learn about the business owners themselves. What kind of education do they have? How long have they been in business and what are their individual strengths and weaknesses? Knowing this, you can **better anticipate** how they might respond to a given situation.

Also, consider the impact of a new competitor entering the marketplace.

A national chain may not have entered your marketplace yet, but what if they do? What will happen to your business if another company who is currently in the marketplace decides to change their focus or expand their offerings and compete directly with you?

Talking To My Competition's Customers

Engaging your competition's customers in real dialogue about what works for them and what doesn't could be the beginning of a long-lasting relationship provided you are able to **meet their needs.**

Some questions you may want to ask them:
- Why do they buy from them?
- Do they have an exceptional product or service?
- Do they happen to be geographically situated in a prime location?
- Maybe the product or service is only mediocre, but they provide exceptional customer experiences?
- Are there things they dislike about the company or is there a product or service they wish that company would provide?

Market Price Awareness

There are many different reasons for how you set your pricing and we could write an entire book just on that one topic. However, the most important element you need to know is what your market will bear in terms of price.

This can easily be found out by researching what kinds of people are doing business with your competitors. Looking at the price they are paying will give you an idea of what price those demographic groups are willing and able to pay.

Knowing this, you can compare the data against your own market demographic to find out what price range would be most appropriate.

Based on this information and depending on your current situation in the market, you could:

- Price lower than your competitors in order to gain market share more quickly;
- Price equal to your competitors with a service or product quality differentiation;
- Price higher than your competition in order to position yourself as a high value product or service;
- Time your promotions to either coincide (you have a lower price) with your competitors or pre-empt (advertise before with similar price) to take the wind out of their program.

The pricing game is all about getting the most **bang** for your marketing buck.

You can advertise until the cows come home, but if your price is out to lunch, then you will be wasting your effort and your cash. Play the game correctly by paying attention to what is going on around you, and you can be that "pain in the side" of the competition whether they are the retailer around the corner or the big box boys in suburbia!

Market Place Awareness

There are literally tens, if not hundreds of thousands of businesses in your marketplace who are all competing for a finite amount of customer spending. As a business owner you must be aware of what is going on in the marketplace, not just in your unique segment. You must take a holistic view of everything that is going on around you as it can have an impact on your bottom line.

- *Is a competitor launching a new product or service?*

- *Is a big box store coming to town?*
- *Is there a new blockbuster movie about to launch or a major sporting event coming to your area?*
- *Has there been a shift (up or down) in real estate prices?*

All of these things—and so many more—could potentially affect your business in the short and long terms. If you have a store front, then a regular **drive around the neighborhood** is a great way to look for clues. If you have an Internet based business, then a regular **surf around the web** is the ticket. What tactics are other businesses who are not specifically in your market doing to improve their marketing? All too often entire industries put their blinders on and chase each other around a similar tactic.

 Having tunnel vision and only focusing on what your direct competitor's are doing to improve their position in the marketplace will keep you too narrowly focused when it comes to trying to make your own improvements.

Take the blinders off and **take a look** at what is going on around you. Look at any and every industry you can to see what they are doing well and what they are doing poorly.

Taking ideas from other industries and being the first to apply them in your market will help you **stay ahead** of your competition and will position you as a leader in the minds of your customers and prospects.

Doing regular market checks is most effective when it becomes habitual. Every time you are out shopping or surfing the web or receiving a telemarketing call, you should keep your mind wide open for opportunities …

 ## Exercise:

1. Identify two of your direct competitors.
2. What advantages do they have over you?
3. In what ways is their offering different to your own?
4. In what ways does the experience of working with you differ than it does working with them?
5. What do they do well?
6. What do they do poorly?
7. What strategies from a completely different industry can you use to enhance your business?

Download the Competitor Analysis worksheet at: www.MakeMyMarketingWorkBook.com.

What You Focus On EXPANDS!

If you spend all your time checking up on the competition, chasing them around and trying to "one-up" them at every turn, your efforts will have the undesirable effect of creating stagnation in your business.

That being said, it is imperative that you spend some time staying on top of what they are doing so that you always have a sense of what could impact your business and what trends you may need to catch up on.

A much more important habit to develop is to **pay attention** to the marketplace in general, regardless of which marketplace you're in.

Remember...

Whether you're shopping at the mall, a grocery store, a big box retailer or a small mom-and-pop shop; whether you're out for dinner, at the movies or traveling for business or pleasure; pay attention to what people are doing.

Become aware as a consumer of the experience you are having and use what you learn in your own business.

Did you get really great customer service at the restaurant after you found a hair in your soup? Or maybe the food was absolutely excellent but the service was merely okay, leaving you feeling a little unsatisfied with the experience overall. Either way, use your knowledge and see how you can **apply it** in your own business.

TIME OUT!
(Pause, Breath, Review)

You now have some great intelligence on your marketplace and the competitive landscape.

You can see how it's important to be very aware of who your customers are. Equally, you have a great understanding of the competition you face.

Finally, to tie it together you have become more aware of your price and place in the market.

SECTION 3 :: My Marketing Message

In This Section You Will:

✓ Learn how to create an exciting and compelling marketing message.

✓ Understand the meaning and importance of having a compelling USP for your business.

✓ Learn how to describe your products and services in terms of the Features, Advantages and Benefits.

✓ Understand how to effectively deliver your message to your target markets to maximize marketing ROI.

✓ Discover the advantages and limitations of traditional advertising, so you can avoid costly mistakes.

✓ Learn the importance of public relations as an integrated part of your overall marketing strategy.

✓ Learn what Guerrilla Marketing is and why it is so powerful.

✓ Look at ways to apply guerrilla marketing to your business.

✓ Learn the basics of direct response internet marketing.

✓ Outline an online marketing strategy using PPC, blogs, YouTube, Facebook, Twitter and more!

Creating A Message

When speaking to your clients in any of the ways you may be conducting business (via the phone, internet, bricks and mortar retail store, advertisements, etc), it is important to maintain a strong sense of continuity across all touch points or the ways in which your customers experience not only your product or service, but your company as a whole.

Your message is **your first impression.** It is how you begin to build rapport with your customers ...

51

Failing to maintain this sense of continuity leaves your customers confused, discombobulated and dissatisfied. Eventually, unless your product is so strong that it can outweigh all the negatives, this lack of continuity will result in a lost customer. Even then, they will simply go elsewhere for a comparable product.

My Unique Selling Proposition (USP)

Before we actually develop a USP for your business, it is important to get an understanding of what it actually means to have a USP.

A USP is not simply a tagline you use in your advertising, or a sales pitch designed to get business. It is an element of your company that sets you apart from the competition. **Something unique** (thus the U) that only you can offer and stand behind.

Legendary marketing giant *Jay Abraham* puts it this way:

> *"A USP is that distinct and appealing idea that sets you and your business favorably apart from every other generic competitor. Your long-term marketing and operational successes will, ultimately, be helped or hurt by the USP you decide upon."*

Please notice that there are two sides to Jay's definition, the USP can either help or hurt your business.

How could a USP hurt your business? Well, let's take a look:

Say you own an internet support company that claims a unique position of answering trouble tickets within 2 hours. Great, but your average response time is actually 3 days... Not cool!

Make sure your USP is something that your company delivers consistently and can continue to deliver to avoid falling short on your most important marketing promise.

To avoid a marketing disaster, don't base your position in the marketplace on a USP that is either unachievable or expensive to deliver and therefore not sustainable. The SMART goal setting rules apply here, with emphasis on the A (Attainable) and R (Realistic).

Said differently, your USP should identify, with laser focus, the way in which your product, service or company is different from the competition. It should directly answer the question, "Why should I do business with you?"

Here are some examples of strong USP statements that successfully answer this question:
- **Domino's Pizza:** "You get fresh, hot pizza delivered to your door in 30 minutes or less—or it's free".
- **FedEx:** "When your package absolutely has to get there overnight".
- **M&M's:** "The milk chocolate melts in your mouth, not in your hand".

When you order a pizza do you expect it to arrive cold, stale and two hours after you've placed the order? Of course not, but Domino's Pizza successfully promises you exactly what you would expect and makes a guarantee that their competition wasn't matching when it was introduced. It's not complicated but it works.

When you order "overnight delivery" do you expect it to arrive three days later? With their USP, FedEx shows you that they are as committed to getting your package delivered as you are. Do they have other cheaper options than overnight delivery? You bet! Not everyone needs to get their package to its destination by the next day or wants to pay premium prices to get it there. But if you do, FedEx stands behind their USP.

These USPs all successfully answer the question, "Why should I do business with you?" and give the customer a sense of confidence that the product will live up to their expectations and that the company will stand behind their promises.

 Exercise:

Pick 2 options within your company that could serve as the basis as potential USPs. Service based options are the simplest route, but if you have a product that does amazing things, then feel free to use it.

Next, brainstorm several guarantees you could offer if you DO fall short for some reason. Free pizza and free delivery are how Dominos & FedEx back up their promises.

Download the USP worksheet at:
www.MakeMy MarketingWorkBook.com.

Remember, this is a work in progress, so it's ok if you don't get it 100% perfect first time round.

Features, Advantages & Benefits are FAB!

Most of the time, people could care less about your product or service, or even you as an individual or organization. What they really want to know is what it can do for them— what problem it will solve or how it will bring them more time, money, fame or even more power and sex!

It's the **emotional attachment** to what you have to offer that creates the need for the customer to purchase your product or service.

Too often organizations focus on the product features; the observable characteristics of the product or service they are selling. This does not motivate your prospect to buy from you! In fact, when it comes to consumer products and services, spending more time than is absolutely necessary outlining the features of your offering (this amount of time varies from product to product), the less likely you are going to be able to close the sale.

This varies somewhat with B2B companies who may need to spend more time on features due to the more practical nature of their purchases. Ultimately though, how a product solves a problem that makes the buying business more profitable or effective will ultimately determine whether or not the sale is made.

The features of a thermal coffee mug might be that it has an open sided handle, an easy to unscrew lid, dual thermal layering, a rubber grip on the outside of the casing, etc.

The advantages are what the features actually do or the service that it performs. For example, the open sided handle and easy to screw off lid make for easy handling and refilling, while the dual thermal layering keeps your drink hotter for a longer period of time and the rubber grip gives you added comfort and reliability.

Outlining the advantages goes one step further towards explaining the **full value** of your product or service, but it doesn't quite get us the whole way.

The benefit of the features (the characteristics of your product or service) and the advantages (the service or function of each feature) must combine to give a **real payoff** to the buyer.

In the case of the thermal coffee mug, the overall benefit is that you get to enjoy your favorite no foam, extra whip, shot of vanilla, soy latte with a dash of cinnamon every sip without having to gulp it down.

And of course with that sleek design, you will look stylish doing it and the rubber grip means you won't spill it all over yourself and look foolish in front of your co-workers!

 Exercise:

List 3 features of your product or service. Then list 3 advantages of each feature. Finally, list 3 benefits of each feature.

Download the FAB worksheet at: www.MakeMy MarketingWorkBook.com.

Emotionally Describe My Product/Service

Communicating with your customers and prospects happens at many different levels and in many different ways. Verbal, auditory and specific past experiences all color how your message is perceived and interpreted.

Different things are important to different people and saying the wrong thing at the wrong time will make your potential customer run for the hills faster than you can say, "Would you like fries with that?"

Say the right thing at the right time and you could have the next pet rock!

The words, colors and specific examples, as well as a customer's direct experience with your company all affect how you are perceived. It can take a lifetime to build a positive image of your business or company in the minds of your customers and it can all be destroyed with a single lapse in good judgment by you or someone on your team.

When describing your product or service to your customers, remember to always make **them** the focal point. Their own needs are what they care about, not how innovative you were in developing your latest widget.

Their emotional connection to what they see as a problem that needs to be solved or a desire that needs to be satiated is what really matters most.

Remember to speak directly to that emotional need by focusing on the benefits and you will persuade more people to do business with you more often.

Exercise:

Take your Features, Advantages and Benefits from the previous exercise and write an emotional and customer focused description of your product. For example:

"With Ethel Stein's Wonder Mug, you will be able to enjoy your favorite hot beverage for up to a full hour. Ethel's patented dual thermal layer heat core keeps your coffee, tea or hot chocolate at just the right drinking temperature so you never have to worry about burning your lip or reaching for your tasty beverage halfway through your long commute and finding it stone cold. Never be disappointed and left out in the cold again."

Don't forget the USP ...
"With The Wonder Mug, we guarantee a consistent temperature for up to 1 hour or your money back!"

Download the FAB worksheet at:
www.MakeMy MarketingWorkBook.com.

WISGAT (What Is So Good About That?)

What is so good about that? Or, more directly, "So what?" It's one of the questions that is always going to come up in the minds of your customers and prospects. Knowing the answer will help you identify and separate the features from the benefits. Anytime you begin to discuss a feature or advantage of your product, you need to be able to answer this question.

WIIFM (What Is In It for Me?)

What's in it for me? Why would I want to do / buy / have what you're offering? Even when your prospect is ready to make a buying decision there is still going to be some hesitancy, particularly if this is your first interaction together. They need to feel as though they are benefiting beyond their expectations by making the decision to purchase from you.

Reviewing My Messaging

Reviewing your marketing message on a regular basis is key to ensuring that you are saying exactly what you want to say—and that it is being interpreted in the correct manner by your customers and prospects.

Are your competitors telling a different story? What, if anything, are they saying about you (or your claimed advantages) in order to downplay your position in the marketplace? Are the needs of your customers being fully met? Did you change something about your product or service that warrants a new or revised message?

Review all of your marketing messages on a quarterly basis to see if they need to be updated or improved. Do not change them just for the sake of changing them as this will result in a definite sense of inconsistency. But don't hold on to something that isn't working either.

Delivering My Message

 Now that you have identified your primary and secondary target audiences and honed your message details, it's time to get the word out to the world!

It's important to realize that, at this point, generating qualified leads is all you're trying to do. You are **creating awareness** of your product or service within the marketplace that you've identified as being most receptive and asking them to "put their hand up" by expressing interest in your offer.

Simply stated - you're going after the low hanging fruit, the people who are already looking for what you have to offer.

At the same time you will be informing those people, who don't yet know, that they have a need that you can fill. As we learned previously, these people come in two varieties:
1. Those who need your product or service but don't yet realize it.
2. Those who don't yet need your product or service, but who may need it at some point in the future.

Although there are literally **hundreds, if not thousands** of different ways to promote your business, they all fall into one of five major categories, which are:
1. **Advertising**
2. **Direct Response**
3. **Public Relations** (also known as PR)
4. **Guerrilla Marketing**
5. **Internet Marketing**

Advertising

Advertising is, in short, a paid communication through a medium such as television, radio, magazines, newspapers, the internet, direct mail and billboards. The sponsor of the advertisement is identified and the message is tightly controlled.

Advertisements can be seen in almost every area of modern society: from product placement in popular movies and television programs to grocery cart seat flaps; from park benches to fully wrapped public buses; from in-store public address announcements to on-hold messages. **Ads scream at you from every direction!** As the consumer, you can't avoid them. As the advertiser, how do you make sure your message is the one that hits home amongst all the others?

There are many arguments for and against the dramatic increase in public space advertising but there is one thing that we can likely all agree on—advertising is not going away any time soon.

For many small to medium-sized businesses trying to **grow their profits,** paid advertising is often not a viable option because of the high cost and low response rate for single ads. To **be truly effective,** a long-term advertising campaign that spans multiple mediums in your target market's usage profile must be undertaken.

That being said, if you've got the money to execute a complete advertising campaign, it can absolutely deliver powerful results over the long term.

Mass Media Advertising

The use of mass media advertising is designed to reach as wide an audience as possible with a message of mass appeal. Of course, as with all good marketing, messages are targeted to markets who are most likely interested in the product or service offering, based on the demographic and psychographic profile of the viewer, listener or reader. This profiling increases the likelihood of generating a **positive response.**

Popular forms of mass media advertising include television, radio, magazines, newspapers, industry periodicals and yellow page ads. Paid advertising online is fast becoming a mainstay in the marketing plans of large and small companies alike.

Each can be seen to target a specific niche audience.

Television, radio and newspapers can be targeted regionally or nationally, depending on the location served by the advertiser, but that's not the only consideration.

The sports section of a newspaper may be more relevant than the new homes section if the advertisement features the grand opening of a new sporting goods outlet store. Similarly, specific TV channels, shows and time segments are targeted for certain types of products based on the viewer profile.

Magazines, periodicals or industry journals might be targeted to reach a specific niche audience. Since these are typically paid for products in a niche area, the readership is much more likely to **be responsive** to an advertisement that directly relates to the content of the publication.

Lastly, yellow pages are regionally targeted and tend to last for an entire year. Although not every person in a given area is a suitable target prospect for your product or service, advertising in the local yellow pages directory creates a **visibility and accessibility** that lasts for an entire year and is available 24/7/365!

Online yellow page listing will likely soon eliminate the physical books, so make sure that your listing is visible in both online and offline publications.

In most areas there is more than one choice for yellow pages providers. Do your homework and make sure it's the one that people use most.

Direct Response Marketing

Direct response marketing, also known as direct marketing, has a simple intent - to elicit a direct and quantifiable response from the person to whom the message is delivered.

One of the most common forms of direct response marketing is the television infomercial. Through an elongated presentation, often 30- to 60-minutes in length, the infomercial viewers **respond directly** and immediately via telephone or internet with their credit card in hand.

The primary intention is not to persuade the consumer to visit their local retail store to view the product or to establish or reinforce a particular company or product

brand, as with most traditional advertising. It is to get the consumer to take action and make a purchase immediately. "CALL NOW—OPERATORS ARE STANDING BY!"

Direct response strategies can (and should) also be used in more traditional forms of advertising, including magazines, newspapers and, more recently, by email and through pay-per-click advertising online. Online direct response efforts are often much **cheaper to produce**, generally speaking, than a television infomercial or mass media advertisement, so even though the response rates may be lower, the return on investment can actually be much higher.

Regular television commercials, unlike infomercials, typically do not try to elicit an immediate response from the viewer. Instead they try to establish or reinforce the **brand identity** of the product or service in question.

Other examples of direct marketing include:
- Door hangers
- Package inserts
- Email advertisements
- Website banner ads
- Newspaper or magazine inserts
- Post cards/mail pieces
- Coupon books
- Parking lot flyers

Database Marketing

Database marketing differs in a slight, yet profound way from normal direct response marketing. That difference lies in the **personalization** of the marketing message to the person who is receiving it.

In direct-response marketing the message is delivered in such a way as to be **suitable to all audiences**. A television infomercial cannot be customized for each individual viewer.

In database marketing however, the specific recipient can be addressed by name and references to their demographic information or psychographic preferences can be made throughout the delivery of the advertisement. Examples of this include direct mail and telemarketing.

More recently, email marketing has **leveraged the power** of database marketing, since database segments can be specifically extracted based on a pre-defined set of criteria and the message personalized to the recipient.

Elements Of A Successful Advertisement

Here are legendary ad-man *Joe Sugarman's* required elements of an advertisement. These elements should be incorporated in essentially any marketing communication with only slight modifications to fit the specific delivery mechanism.

(Joe sold, among many other things, over 20 million pairs of BluBlocker sunglasses via direct response marketing tactics.)

1. **Headline** – To get your attention and draw you to the sub-headline.

2. **Sub-headline** – To give you more information and further explain the attention-getting headline.

3. **Photo or drawing** – To get your attention and to illustrate the product more fully.

4. **Caption** – To describe the photo or drawing. This element is often overlooked but is one that is very often read.

5. **Copy** – To convey the main selling message for your product or service.

6. **Paragraph headings** – To break the copy into chunks, making it look less imposing to the reader.

7. **Logo** – To display the name of the company selling the product.

8. **Price** – To let the reader know what the product or service costs. It can be in large type or buried in the copy.

9. **Response device** – To get the reader a way to respond to the ad, by using a coupon, calling a toll-free number or other ordering information. This is usually found near the end of the ad.

10. **Overall layout** – To provide the overall appearance for the ad, by using effective graphic design.

Each and every element of an ad is meant to do one thing and one thing only—get the reader to **read the first sentence.**

That sentence, in turn, pulls you in to the next sentence and on through the copy the reader goes.

Though very different in nature, television and radio ads follow very much the same format, except that they are incredibly focused due to the limitation of message length. As previously mentioned, the above required elements can be applied to any marketing communications message.

Though it may be easy to second guess or dispute the above feature-set of a successful advertisement, it is difficult to dispute Joe Sugarman's success in the marketplace.

 Exercise:

Create three headlines you can test in your advertising. Remember that your headline should be catchy and attention-grabbing. Its purpose is to get the reader further into the ad.

Now, create a sub-headline for each headline that gives a little more explanation and draws the reader in further.

Next, develop five bullet points that you can use as paragraph headers to break up the copy and grab your readers' attention.

And finally, you need a response device. How will readers of your ad respond? Will they call, fax, clip a coupon or visit your website or retail store?

Download the Advertisement worksheet at: www.MakeMyMarketingWorkBook.com.

Public Relations—Perception Is Reality ...

Public Relations (PR) is one of the most powerful forms of marketing communications. The media can affect the way your company is perceived by the marketplace and additional weight is given in the **mind of the consumer** to messages delivered in this medium, since it is seen as being "reported" instead of "advertised".

Consumers expect you to make bold claims and great offers in an advertisement. Yet, when they read a story that features your business as a solution to a problem they have or desire they can relate to, then they are much more likely to accept the claims you make since they are being reported by what they perceive to be an impartial and reliable source.

From a marketing perspective, this is a very powerful thing indeed and should definitely be tapped and used to maximum advantage. Not only is it a pervasive form of communications, it is also very cost effective.

At its most basic, the core essence of PR is about successfully managing your reputation. It is the result of **what you do and say,** and conversely, what others say about you.

At its most complex, PR is the subtle art of public persuasion, used to influence public opinion and, ultimately, **behavior**.

Like all marketing communications efforts, your PR should be a strategically planned, consistent and sustained effort over the long term. The aim? To raise your profile, affirm and solidify your firm's expertise, product quality, pedigree of personnel and inform the public about your contribution to the community. You will also want to use PR to popularize your successes, downplay any failures and announce changes.

Watch The News, To Be In The News

If you want to be in the news, whether you are an established business (and therefore easily perceived as an expert) or you're just getting started and need to **develop your reputation,** you must watch the news and know what is wanted or needed.

That's worth repeating: **If you want to be in the news, you must watch the news and know what is wanted or needed.**

You can do this in various ways, depending on the medium. The obvious first step is to pay attention to the stories that are currently being run. Look for trends as well as unique and interesting ways that you can hook the current media buzz into your own business.

Most media channels have websites and often list their upcoming programming and editorial calendars. You can also go the old fashioned route and call them up and ask them what they need.

In order to be selected by the media, you must have an interesting or relevant story to tell and you must have an audience that wants to hear it. Much like advertising, there is little point in discussing your new brand of cat food on the "All About Dogs" segment.

Give Them What They Want!

When sending information to the media that you want them to consider for an upcoming story, make sure you send it in a format that they want to receive! Usually this comes in the form of a press release or a media kit.

A press release is a written statement distributed directly to the media. It is a **fundamental tool** of public relations. Press releases are often communicated by a newswire service to news media. However, if you really want yours to be read, it is advisable to send it specifically to the journalist you expect to cover your story.

If you've **done your research** properly, you should know who the specific journalist is who will likely be reporting on this story, because it fits with their regular assignments. You should make an advance call to let them know it is coming, send the release directly to them, and then follow up by phone to ensure that they received it and to see if they want to pursue the story.

 Exercise:

List one specific PR opportunity that is targeted to your primary audience for each of the following: Television; Radio; Newspaper; Magazine.

Download the PR worksheet at:
www.MakeMy MarketingWorkBook.com.

How To Write A Press Release

The correct format for a press release isn't complicated. Just like in a written ad, you need an **attention getting heading** to sell your story and of course it must answer the six basic questions of:

Who, what, where, when, why, ... and of course, how?

Put yourself in the shoes of the journalist when you are writing your press release and you will gain a clearer understanding of what you should write about. Read or watch other news items and see if you can spot each of these six basic questions.

Journalists write in a style called the inverted pyramid, so your press releases should follow the same format. Essentially what this means is that the foundation of the story—the majority of the details and **interesting information** is provided at the top. Although this may seem contrary to any writing you may have done in other areas, it seems to work for journalists, so make sure you stick with it.

Here are the essential elements, in order of appearance, of a successful press release:

1. **FOR IMMEDIATE RELEASE** – This tells the journalist that they can use the story right away and that the information is not embargoed (to be

held for a future release date). Failing to include this will likely mean that your press release is thrown in the trash since reporters are not willing to risk leaking an embargoed news item ahead of its scheduled release date.

2. **Headline** - Used to grab the attention of journalists and briefly summarize the news.

3. **Dateline** - Contains the release date and usually the originating city of the press release.

4. **Introduction** - First paragraph in a press release, that generally gives basic answers to the questions of who, what, when, where and why.

5. **Body** - Further explanation, statistics, background, or other details relevant to the news. You should usually provide a specific quote from an officer of the company within this portion of the press release.

6. **Boilerplate** - Generally a short "about" section, providing independent background on the issuing company, organization, or individual.

7. **Close** - In North America, traditionally the symbol "-30-" appears after the boilerplate or body and before the media contact information, indicating that the release is ending. A more modern equivalent has been the "###" symbol.

8. **Media Contact Information** - Name, phone number, email address, mailing address, or other contact information for the PR or other media relations contact person.

See, not so complicated is it? Just follow the format and you will be getting free press in no time!

Download a free sample press release template at www.MakeMyMarketingWorkBook.com.

A Quick Word About Online PR

With the explosion of people using the internet for all manner of information gathering, the use of public relations online has grown right along with it.

While **the fundamentals** are the same, there are a few added benefits to utilizing online public relations as part of your overall PR strategy.

First, since the major search engines, and Google in particular, rank the value of your website (and, therefore, where you end up in the search results) in part based on the value they already place on the websites you're associated with, the use of online press releases can greatly improve your **search engine optimization** efforts (we'll talk more about that very soon), driving targeted traffic to your website.

By linking keywords from within your press release to relevant pages on your website, members of the media and general public alike can link directly to your site from right within your release. The power of this cannot be understated for two primary reasons.

The first is that online news agencies are quickly gaining ground on the major offline news sources. Trends indicate that online news agencies (such as Yahoo! News, Google

News and MSN) could eventually overtake traditional outlets. Whether or not that actually happens, the current reality is that **millions of people** now get their news through online portals and those portals pick their news stories and copy them directly from the online wire services! That includes the embedded links back to your site, which further increases the amount of available traffic and value ranking provided by the search engines.

The second reason is that many consumers now go directly to these online newswire services to peruse stories of interest to them without waiting for them to be picked up by the online news agencies. Consumers are now directly empowered to search out and find their own news—and many of them are more than happy to reprint your press release on their blog or website, if it is of value or interest to their readers. This again drives additional traffic and value ranking for your site.

Develop A Media Kit

A media kit is an essential component in attracting and solidifying media coverage. Your kit contains information and materials presented in a **compelling fashion** that gives readers insight into you and your business.

It goes without saying that your media kit should be professionally written and well organized so that it is **easy for the reader** to extract the important and relevant facts.

There is much opinion about how to put a media kit together, particularly from a design point of view, however the following basic elements should always be included.

After the basics are covered, then you can personalize your kit as you see fit:

1. **Cover letter** – In typical business letter format it explains the intent for sending the media kit, and is customized for the specific recipient. It also provides information on how to contact you for more information.

2. **Backgrounder** – This is a summary of your company including the history and any important information you wish to share. It should explain when the company was founded, the products or services you offer, any new company developments that may be of interest, the number of corporate offices you have and the location of your headquarters (if appropriate) and any awards you have received.

3. **Biographies** – Write-ups of key personnel, their history and how they started with your company. Additional information such as education, past experience, where they are from, community involvement and any personal awards or recognitions can also be included.

4. **Press Release** – Only your most recent 1-2 press releases should be included.

5. **Media Coverage** – All press received for your business can be scanned or photocopied and inserted into this section. Dates should be listed next to the media coverage your business has received.

6. **Testimonials** – These should be gathered from your best and most satisfied clients and included with copies of any complimentary letters you received.

7. **Business Card** – It is amazing how many people forget to include this key item. Remember—People can easily keep your business card in a rolodex separately from your media kit.

Other items that you may wish to include are: company brochure, photos of key personnel, list of **key questions** with answers for reporters, suggested interview topics, catalog of products, industry news, published writing and press passes.

The design and layout of your media kit should be put together in a way that reflects your company brand. If your business is selling chocolate chip cookies, you want something that is light and delicious, not something overly corporate.

It is important to also have a digital version of your media kit available on your website. You never know when a member of the media will visit your site looking for information on a story they are working on.

If your information is readily available, it could mean the difference between being featured in the story and being overlooked entirely.

Guerrilla Marketing—Not Gorilla!

Jay Conrad Levinson popularized the term "guerrilla marketing" in 1983 when he published a book by the same name. Since that time, guerrilla marketing has become a marketing catch phrase, particularly for small businesses looking to **maximize their marketing** efforts with little or no money.

Why "guerrilla" marketing?

Guerrilla fighters, in terms of actual physical conflict, are a body of fighters who engage in non-standard or irregular warfare. Essentially, their tactics are outside the bounds of traditional battle.

As a small business owner, you are, in a sense, at war every time you go to market with a product or service. You're at war with your direct competition, your indirect competition and your variable competition. In business, as in warfare, it is imperative that you discover all opportunities and advantages that are available to you and then proceed to **systematically exploit** those advantages to the best of your ability.

Guerrilla marketing then is the use of unconventional promotional activities that require a much smaller budget than more conventional marketing activities. In fact, one of the precepts of guerrilla marketing, according to Levinson, is "achieving conventional goals, such as profits and joy, with unconventional methods, such as investing energy instead of money."

It is this idea of **"investing energy instead of money"** that is one of the primary measures determining if a marketing tactic is guerrilla or not.

Another defining element of Guerrilla Marketing is the tendency to **respond to change** instead of resist it.

Guerrillas see what is without tryingtochangeitandaretherefore able to adapt and respond to the changing landscape while other more traditional competitors resist the changes and suffer the consequences of not adapting.

The music industry is a prime example of a traditional industry that was not able, as a whole, to adapt to the changes brought about by the popularity of the internet, high-speed access and file sharing programs.

Instead of finding a way to adapt and respond to this major change in landscape, many of the major labels have instead resisted and tried to enforce outdated rules. Musicians who **embrace the new landscape** have not only gained new fans who are more than willing to pay for their music, they are reaching new fans and filling venues the world over.

A recent case is 16-year-old Canadian pop/R&B musician Justin Bieber who posted videos of himself playing guitar and singing on YouTube and landed a major record deal because of the massive amounts of attention his videos were attracting.

Examples of Guerrilla Marketing Tactics

One of the greatest things about guerrilla marketing is that it is literally being defined and redefined on a day-to-day, week-to-week basis. That being said, here are some examples of guerrilla marketing tactics you can employ in your business:

Create a killer customer experience – This is probably the most efficient and effective form of guerrilla marketing and it can be implemented by any business. Create an experience that revolves around the customer and which is extremely memorable and people won't be able to help but talk about your company.

Collaborate vs. Compete – In the new world of social marketing, collaboration is key in generating successful cross-marketing campaigns. Have a look at what other businesses outside your specific marketplace your customers frequent.

Once you've identified possible collaborators, you can approach them with a joint venture or strategic alliance proposal that will increase value for both parties.

For example, you sell golf equipment through a retail store. Partner with someone offers golfing lessons to cross-promote each other. You can each give a coupon or other advertisement for the other party at the point of purchase or create a formal combination of both products that services the end client in a more complete way.

Develop a Referral Program - Whether you pay your clients to refer you to others or not, having a formal system by which you ask your clients to refer new business to you is a key way to build new leads and grow your business.

Generally speaking, if someone is happy with the service or product they are getting from you, they will likely know others who could also benefit from doing business with you. Asking your customers for referrals is an absolute necessity for any business.

Rewarding them for generating new leads for you, particularly if that lead **results in a sale,** is always a good idea. You can reward them by offering a free gift, a discount off a future purchase or even by giving them a cash commission.

Good Old Fashioned "Word of Mouth" – These marketing messages transferred primarily in a face-to-face environment, but increasingly by social networking online, SMS (text) messages, email and blog postings, are the oldest form of marketing.

Often referred to as "viral" marketing, word of mouth campaigns are based around ideas and materials that are easily spread throughout a community of **like-minded consumers.** When orchestrating a viral marketing campaign it is important to target the "sneezers"—people who will naturally spread your message to others—so that the message is spread quickly through a given network.

Sticker campaigns – paste them everywhere and anywhere that your target audience will see them (use removable stickers to avoid creating a negative response).

Consumer reports – they should edutain (educate and entertain) your prospects while reinforcing the benefits of using your product or service.

Seminars – Another form of "edutainment", a live seminar can teach consumers more about a given subject of interest, while also informing them of an available product or service.

Business cards – A business staple, cards that successfully utilize both sides and include a strong call-to-action have proven to increase awareness and generate leads.

Networking – Attend networking events that are frequented by other professionals in your community and you can generate leads as well as joint venture and strategic alliance relationships.

Write a column – Identify a local or national publication that serves your target audience and pitch a recurring column in your area of expertise.

T-shirt campaign – Owners, staff and "street teams" alike can all wear branded t-shirts or golf shirts during regular activities to create awareness and recognition of a brand or product.

Podcast or Internet Radio Show – What information could you record (in audio and/or video) and then broadcast through one of the many "new media" distribution methods online to attract and educate your prospects?

Exercise:

List the number one way you will leverage guerrilla marketing tactics in each of the following areas: **Customer Experience; Collaboration; Word of Mouth / Referrals.**

Now spend 10 minutes brainstorming additional low-cost, high-visibility ways you can promote your business.

Download the Guerrilla Marketing worksheet at: www.MakeMyMarketingWorkBook.com.

Internet Marketing

The popularization of the internet at the consumer level has given small businesses a huge advantage over larger corporations when it comes to implementing **new strategies** and taking advantage of the rapid rate of development in the online community.

These days literally anyone can produce a high quality Internet campaign, for a **fraction of the cost** it would take to produce a similar offline campaign. And thanks to companies like Google, Yahoo, and MSN, the playing field of internet advertising has been leveled. By offering targeted, localized advertising to small-and medium-sized businesses, ROI has grown while the bottom line has been lowered.

The evolutionary step, popularized in the last few years by Google Adwords®, is to refine the ad delivery to those consumers specifically searching keywords related to your product or service. Done correctly you can access your **ultimate target market** with just a few key strokes. Even 10 years ago, access to target audiences like this would have cost you thousands of dollars and countless man-hours. Now you can get started for just a few hundred dollars or less.

Unlike traditional advertising, your ads are only seen by people who are already searching for what you're selling. This self-selection process delivers a **higher quality lead** to your electronic doorstep.

Once the consumer has chosen your company, and entered your e-store, the design of your website will determine the online to offline or e-commerce conversion rates.

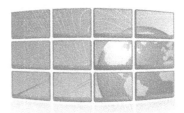 Just to make sure we're clear, while internet marketing can cover any facet of online marketing, current use of the term commonly refers to the use of direct response marketing strategies that were traditionally used in direct mail, radio, and TV infomercials, now applied to the internet business space. It's taking **ad space to cyber space.**

Direct response marketing methods have been found to be particularly useful on the internet due to its tracking capabilities coupled with the ability to instantly reach the prospect, **anywhere in the world,** at any time of the day, whether it be business-to-business or business-to-consumer.

Think about it! Your customers have **24 hour access** to your products and services.

> *Can't sleep? Shop online!*
>
> *Don't want to stand in the rain? Shop on line!*
>
> *Want to research a product without going to the mall? Shop on-line!*

Consumers can log onto the internet and learn about products, as well as purchase them, at any hour without you paying for staff, lights or even up front inventory.

Overall, internet marketing can help build a local business while enabling you to expand from a local market to both national and international marketplaces overnight. The web provides access like no other time in the history of commerce!

As mentioned above, it levels the playing field for big and small players. Unlike traditional marketing media (like print, radio and TV), entry into the realm of internet marketing can be a lot less expensive, allowing small businesses to **compete directly** with their larger, more well-established competitors.

And while we're at it, since exposure, response and overall efficiency of digital media is much easier to track than that of traditional "offline" media, internet marketing offers a greater **sense of accountability** for advertisers. They know exactly how much bang they are getting for their buck!

Compared to the other media marketing (like print, radio and TV), internet marketing is growing very fast. It's also gaining popularity among small businesses and even consumers. The measurability of the internet as a media **makes it easier** to implement innovative e-marketing tactics that will provide a better Cost Per Acquisition (CPA) than other media.

On a side note, in most countries, internet marketing and advertising spending is only around 5%, but growing. TV, radio, and print on the other hand are more, but declining. So hang on, and get ready to ride the wave!

So ... You Need Your Own Website!

In today's marketplace, having your own website, preferably located at your own domain name (www.YOURCOMPANY. com), is not an option—it is an **absolute necessity.**

 Exercise:

If you do not yet own your own domain name, go online now and see if it is available as a "dot com" domain. Two popular domain sites are: godaddy. com and namecheap.com

If it is, spend the $8 - $10 right now and register the name so that you own it and can start using it. No luck the first time around? Keep looking for variations that work (i.e. "dot net" domains)!

Social Marketing and Web 2.0

You may have heard of Facebook, Twitter and YouTube as well as blogging and podcasting. But have you heard of StumbleUpon, social bookmarking or Vlogging?

What about Squidoo, Technorati, Digg or Del.ic.io.us? No, those are not the names of up and coming R&B Artists, they are the next wave of social networking. And if they were the names of R&B artists, you better believe they would have space on Squidoo, Technorati and Del.ic.io.us!

Social networking and Web 2.0 are **buzz words** but what they describe is as old as human civilization itself— the propensity for humans to congregate in groups with  other like-minded individuals. Internet technology makes this natural tendency very easy and intuitive to implement on a moment-by-moment basis since the internet itself is based on the very same principles.

Using this natural tendency to network by providing valued information free of charge to interested participants can drive enormous amounts of traffic to your business. But more than that, by offering the **ability to collaborate** on an idea, you engage your customer as a peer, making them feel part of your society or inner circle.

One of the simplest ways of leveraging this type of natural human behavior is to install a blog—or "web log"—on your website. By posting regularly to your blog and inviting visitors—**those would be your customers and prospects—**

to join the discussion by commenting on your posts, you reinforce the natural tendency to network in your customers and prospects.

You can start your own blog using any one of a hundred free options currently available online. One of the best is a **free service** provided by Google called Blogger (www.blogger.com). These free blogs are generally hosted at the website that offers them and are separate from your website.

If you are more technically savvy—or if you have a Webmaster who can help you—you can download a powerful blogging system called Wordpress for free. Having your own blog hosted on your site, while a little more difficult to set up, definitely adds to your overall brand strength and credibility. Visit www.wordpress.org for more information.

Want another way to Blog for Business?

Interact with other blogs that are appropriate and relevant to your business by adding your own comments and feedback on other people's posts. DO NOT blatantly advertise or you will get banned from that blog—but if you **use your knowledge and expertise** to provide insightful commentary that is directly related to the post that you are commenting on, you can include a blog signature (similar to your email signature) with a link that will generate traffic back to your site. It's easier than handing out business cards!

Similar to blogs, forums are places where groups of like-minded people congregate online to support, help, complain, gossip, etc. By becoming an active member of forum groups that are topically relevant to your business, and by including a signature on every post, you **create trust** with the people who read your forum posts and can generate traffic through your forum signature link.

Blogging and forum posting also help with Search Engine Optimization (SEO) since the links from other sites, back to your own domain, give added weight to your website ranking with the search engines.

Find related blogs and forums by searching for your specific keywords, plus the word "blog" or "forum". For example, search for "small business marketing blog" and "small business marketing forum".

 Exercise:

Go to your computer, open your browser and launch your preferred search engine.

In the search field type a keyword phrase that is appropriate to your business plus the word "blog".

Example: **small business marketing blog.**

Review the search results and identify at least three blogs that are directly related to your business. Bookmark them or add them to your favorites so that you can find them quickly later.

Repeat this process replacing the word "blog" with the word "forum" in your search.

Create accounts (if necessary) and start interacting with these groups of people. Become a resource by contributing and collaborating. Make sure that you have a blog or forum signature that identifies you and **links to your website.** People who are interested in what you have to say will naturally click through to visit your site. There is no sense in having the conversation without the pay off.

Facebook, Twitter and LinkedIn, Oh My!

In the past several years, the popularity of social networking sites has positively exploded to the point that you should only ignore them at your business peril. Every day, consumers are researching, discussing, recommending and—yes— purchasing products and services through the Internet.

While there are literally hundreds of social networking sites centered around specific niche topics, the big 3 are the places to start in order to get your feet wet and start leveraging the power of social marketing online.

Facebook Isn't Just For Friends Any More ...

Facebook (if you haven't heard) is a social site that allows you to create a profile, add "friends" and share your videos, pictures, current status and more.

You can also "link" your Facebook profile to your blog, if you have one, which will automatically update your Facebook page with new posts to your blog, creating an additional traffic stream back to your website.

It was originally created by Harvard student Mark Zuckerberg to keep in touch with his college friends but has since grown to serve businesses around the globe with means of communicating publicly with their customers and prospects.

On Facebook you can communicate with people by posting comments on their "wall" or by joining groups (very similar to forums) which are based around a specific topic of interest. Or you can choose to start and moderate your own group, if you're up for the task.

Facebook Fan Pages are a new phenomenon and are different from groups in a few key ways.

While you can host a discussion in both Fan Pages and Groups, you can't currently get statistics on your group activity, while you can with Fan Pages. Being able to track the effectiveness of your Facebook efforts is critically important in order to know whether your time online is generating a tangible result for your business (or not).

You can also create relevant "events" within your Fan Page, which you cannot do in a group. (You can create a Facebook event separately from your group, however.)

Finally, and most importantly, Facebook Fan Pages are visible to unregistered users. This means that they are indexed by Google and the other search engines, while groups are only accessible by those people who already have a Facebook account.

But there is a possible negative from creating a Fan Page and that is that the conversation is solely based around

YOU. Done right, you can mitigate this potential risk, but for newbies in the Facebook marketing arena, it may be wise to start by creating a Facebook Group that is based on a topic of unifying interest, then progressively move toward a Fan Page if/when it becomes appropriate.

 Exercise:

Go online to Facebook.com and create an account if you don't already have one.

Next locate the "groups" section and find 3 active groups that are related to your business niche or expertise and join them. Once there, enter the discussion already taking place by adding your input. Even if you disagree, providing you do so without malice, you can engage in lively discussion and position yourself as a knowledgeable expert.

(Just like forums and blogs, you don't want to start spamming the groups with links back to your site without adding to the conversation. Social networking is a longer-term proposition. If you blatantly advertise yourself you will soon find yourself banned from the group, left on the outside looking in.)

While you're logged in, begin researching and planning your Facebook Fan Page. When you've developed a strategic plan (and enough "friends" to share it with) then you can actually go ahead and create it.

Download the Facebook worksheet at
www.Make MyMarketingWorkBook.com.

Twitter And The Rise of Micro Blogging

You've probably heard of "instant messaging" where you and a friend can communicate through one-to-one chat online from anywhere in the world. Twitter takes that a step further, but also a step back.

With its 140 character limit and "What are you doing right now" instant updating, Twitter has taken the world by storm.

Called "micro-blogging" by some, Twitter has gained incredible popularity in business as well as celebrity circles and can be used to enhance your online presence by contributing useful content centered around your primary business expertise.

As "real-time search" capabilities grow (at the time of writing both Facebook and Google are working to include real-time Twitter updates in their search results) platforms like Twitter will become more and more important as a means of communicating with your customers and prospects.

Twitter moves chat forward in the sense that many more than just two or three people can communicate on a single or wide range of topics... and backward in the sense that this conversation is largely visible to the general public and therefore offers an open invitation for others to join the conversation.

This step "backward" is not a bad thing at all since it increases the perceived intimacy between you and your target audience.

 **Insider Tip:**

Know The Rules If You're Going to Play The Game!

Online communication tools are meant to be bi-directional—if you are going to join the conversation then plan to respond to customers through their chosen medium. If someone asks you a question on Twitter then you'd better answer them on Twitter or risk being flamed.

Don't get thousands of followers and then neglect to take care of them or the Twitterverse will hear about it (whether you like what's being said or not!)

Once again, it's important to remember that there is already a conversation taking place in the minds (and mouths) of your prospects and customers and it is your job to enter that conversation gracefully. Do NOT try to interrupt what's already going on with a conversation of your own design.

Just like someone who approaches a group of people at a party and loudly tries to turn the conversation to something they can speak about, people in the social websphere won't appreciate the intrusion.

But if you can enhance the conversation by adding your own unique viewpoint or share your related experience, you'll be welcomed into the fold with open arms.

Exercise:

Go online to Twitter.com and create an account if you don't already have one.

Write up a profile that describes what you do (including a link back your own site) and learn how to customize your Twitter page to support your company's visual brand.

Next, use the search function (search.twitter.com) to find people who are talking about subjects that you are an expert in and which are related to your business goals. Follow those people and pay attention to what they are saying and how they are saying it.

Download the Twitter worksheet at www.MakeMy MarketingWorkBook.com.

Get LinkedIn For Business-to-Business

LinkedIn is a social network designed more for professionals and is a powerful tool for building your professional connections and enhancing your online reputation.

But there are also some little known ways to build your B2C business by interacting through groups and LinkedIn's "Answers" functionality.

Once you've created a profile you can begin finding people you are already connected to and finding new connections to meet and interact with. You can then start joining groups (like the Facebook groups we discussed earlier), which are centered around a particular topic or theme and making use of the "Answers" feature.

LinkedIn Answers are a way to post questions targeted at your ideal prospect or answer questions that have been posted by them. For example, if you offer therapeutic massage services, you might search for the key phrase "therapeutic massage therapy" and answer related questions based on your particular point of view and expertise.

This helps to establish you as an expert, improves your online reputation (since others with similar questions can also see your answer) as well as send targeted traffic back to your website.

LinkedIn now also features "network updates" functionality much like Facebook's status and Twitter's "what are you doing"?

In fact, all of these systems can be interlinked so that when you update one status, all of the others are automatically updated at the same time!

 Exercise:

Go online to LinkedIn.com and create an account if you don't already have one.

Complete your profile following the directions on screen and begin locating people with whom you already have an established relationship and be sure to connect with them immediately.

Ask those you trust to write a recommendation for you, which will further enhance your credibility online if and when someone stumbles across your profile.

Join a few relevant groups and start to get a sense of how people in this community are interacting with each other. You can lurk for awhile while you get used to things or you can join the conversation right away—it's totally up to you.

The last step is to start reviewing the "answers" section and seeing how it works so that you can determine your optimal strategy for using LinkedIn to grow your online reputation and drive targeted traffic back to your website.

Download the LinkedIn worksheet at www.MakeMy MarketingWorkBook.com.

SEO In A Box!

Search Engine Optimization, or SEO, has become a hugely complex topic, so much so that there are complete volumes dedicated tot his one manner of online marketing. But SEO doesn't have to be so complex, at least not at this stage of the game.

Simply put, SEO is about optimizing your website so that the search engines can find and index (list) your website more easily and return your site higher in the SERPs.

A SERP is a **S**earch **E**ngine **R**esults **P**age—the page that is returned when you search for information on your favorite search engine.

Obviously, the closer you are to the top of list, the more organic (free!) search traffic your site is going to get.

Here's basic "SEO in a box". For each unique page on your site:

1. Write copy naturally around **a single topic or keyword** using expert knowledge instead of trying to dump specific keyword phrases over and over again.

2. Use META tags wisely by including keyword and description tags relevant to the specific page content.

3. Use the "alt" description for all images in your website to include contextually relevant keywords.

4. Ensure that you have page title and matching header ("H1") tags on every page that reinforce the page topic and keywords.

5. Get quality inbound links from other sites that are contextually relevant to your business.

Follow these five steps and you will be way ahead of your competition when it comes to SEO. More importantly, you won't break the bank in the process.

Pay Per Click Advertising

Pay-per-click (PPC) was popularized by Google Adwords as a way for small business owners to reach their target market in an affordable fashion. The cost of PPC advertising is exactly what you'd think, based on the name. Each time a prospect **clicks** your ad, you will pay a predetermined fee. You can set your maximum "per click" price that you are willing to pay, as well as a daily or monthly spending limit.

The best thing about PPC advertising, particularly with Google Adwords, is that your ad is only shown when people search for keywords that you specify. So the people who are likely to click your ad are people who searched for keywords that are directly related to your business.

If you've done your job well, the ad speaks directly to the keywords they searched for, as does the page you direct them to. If so, and if you have a quality product or service to offer, then your **conversion rates** will be high and you will get good return on investment.

The rule of thumb here is to test your ROI constantly to ensure that your advertisements are **generating positive cash flow** for your business.

 Exercise:

Go to www.google.com/adwords and sign up for a free account, but don't spend any money just yet!

Google adwords is a powerful tool with tons of features that you need to learn about. For now just create an account and start educating yourself using their huge resource section.

When you're searching online, start to pay attention to the sponsored ads (PPC ads) you see. If they are relevant to your search then go ahead and click them, but don't click them randomly or you will cost some other business owner their well earned money.

Notice whether the ads that are displayed for your search terms work for you as a consumer. Check to see if the ad copy is targeted and relevant to your search phrase. When you click the ad, is the landing page also targeted to both your search phrase AND the ad copy? Is there a call to action that is trying to convert you into a customer?

Pay attention to all of these things when you are browsing the internet, and learn from other people's success!

Email Marketing

Much cheaper than traditional direct mail campaigns, email marketing allows you to be in **instant contact** with your database of prospects and customers.

Email deliverability can present a challenge, as can having your messages filtered out as junk or spam. The best bet is to go with a reliable email-marketing provider to manage your online lists for you. Examples include:

Aweber: http://www.aweber.com/

1 Shopping Cart: http://www.1shoppingcart.com

You can export and back up the information at any time, but since their business is email delivery, you stand a much better chance of getting **more messages through** to your intended recipients.

What's more, they will automatically update their systems to meet with evolving email and spam regulations so that you don't have to stay on top of the current trends.

 Exercise:

Sign up for an email service that will allow you to collect the names and email addresses of your website visitors. Both Aweber and 1ShoppingCart offer cheap trial periods without a full investment.

Next, add a sign-up form to your website that allows users to enter their information in exchange for something of value (a consumer report, free sample or other incentive).

Once you have their email address on file, you can market your product or service to them via email in one of two ways:

a. **Autoresponders** – These are emails that are sent on a predetermined schedule based upon the date on which the user signed up to your list (i.e. an immediate thank you message). The value of an autoresponder series of emails is that it can be created once and then executed automatically when someone new signs up to your list.

b. **Broadcast emails** – These emails are sent on a specific date to your database. It can be anything you wish and is manually scheduled to go out at a certain date and time.

You could offer seasonal sales, special rates for good customers or "reactivation" emails to customers who haven't purchased from you in some time.

◀)) Insider Tip:

It's Not Just What You Say...
Every time you talk about your business, you are delivering your message. Knowing what you want to say and how you want to say it will allow you to feel comfortable in any situation.

Practice what you will say when someone new asks you about your business in front of the mirror once per week. Get comfortable with the words you will use. Just as importantly, at least get familiar with the level of energy you will use when you talk about your business.

The vast majority of communication happens at a non-verbal level, so if your energy level or body language is not aligned with the actual words you are using, people will pick up on it.

TIME OUT!
(Pause, Breath, Review)

You have now developed an **exciting and compelling marketing message**. This message utilizes a strong USP and is able to emotionally connect with your potential clients.

You are fully aware of your product or service **Features, Advantages, and Benefits (FAB)**!

Having created a great message, you've now also looked at many ways to deliver that message. Your marketing is now sprinkled with things such as PPC, SEO, and even a Guerrilla or two.

You'll now also be discussing your Social Marketing and Web 2.0 strategy.... Possibly with someone from the media as part of your PR campaign.

SECTION 4 :: Continue My Marketing

In This Section You Will:

✓ Understand key marketing metrics that you must track in your business.
✓ Develop clear, defined Business Health Indicators (BHIs) to help measure your marketing efforts.
✓ Learn how to accurately tracking your ROMI.
✓ Understand why testing changes to your marketing in isolation is imperative to improving your ROMI over the long term.
✓ Create the basics of a marketing budget and plan out your spending for the next 12 months.
✓ Learn the three primary levels of a front-end marketing funnel.
✓ Develop an up sell, down sell and cross sell program to increase your sales per customer.

Measuring My Marketing

What you focus on expands and what you track is quantifiable. You can have the best marketing program on the planet, but unless you track the impact, and the results how will you know? There is an old marketing adage: "I know 50% of my marketing is effective... I just don't know which half!"

We know measuring or tracking sounds kind of boring, but think of it this way:

Imagine you are at the bank, asking for a credit extension when your Bank Manager says, "So, how is that new marketing program going?" You fidget in your seat for a moment before answering ...

> a. "It's going pretty well. I've done some neat stuff and—It's good—I think?"—Not very convincing...

OR ...

> b. "Well, we've split our efforts evenly between online and offline direct response ads and although it's early in the testing, we are showing 300% growth in our primary target market of women age 30 through 50."

See? **Numbers can be cool!**

Knowing where you want to be as well as where you are right now and then setting clear, definable targets along the way is the surest way to achieve success. On the other hand, not having specific, measurable goals will almost guarantee that you will under-perform.

When planning and executing your marketing efforts it's not enough to just **"do"**. You also have to check to ensure that what you're doing is actually working and giving you the results you desire.

In order to understand if a marketing program is working you need to understand:

- Where you're starting from
- Where you're going
- What you're doing to get there

- How you're going to measure progress to ensure you're on track
- How you are doing in relation to your marketing budget

So, if you've been paying attention so far, you'll have a pretty clear idea by now about the first three things:
- Where you're starting from
- Where you're going
- What you're doing to get there

However, there's a critical part of any successful marketing program that's going to enable you to stay on top of all the **marketing buzz** flying around and that is:
- How you're going to measure progress to ensure you're on track for success
- How you're doing in relation to your marketing budget

This is where Business Health Indicators (BHIs) and a marketing budget come into play.

Business Health Indicators (you may have heard them also called Key Performance Indicators), help you define and measure progress toward the goals you have set for the business. Once you have defined the marketing goals of the business, you need a way to measure where you are in relation to your target at any moment in time. You can then accurately measure your progress toward those goals.

So What Are Business Health Indicators?

BHIs are quantifiable RESULTS, decided and agreed to beforehand, that reflect the critical success factors of your business and different functions within the business.

They will, of course, differ depending on the type of business you run.

For example, your business may have the percentage of revenue from repeat customers as one of its BHIs.

Alternatively, a school may focus its BHIs on the graduation rates, average CPA or job placement rates of its students.

Whatever BHIs you select, they must reflect your business objectives. They must be **key to your success,** and they must be quantifiable (measurable).

BHIs usually are long-term considerations. What we mean by this is that the definition of what they are (what you are looking at) and how you measure them (how you look at it) do not change often. Only the specific goals related to a particular BHI may change as your business goals change, or as you get closer to achieving a goal.

BHIs Must Be Quantifiable

If a BHI that you set is going to be of any value, there must be a way for you to accurately define and measure it.

"Generate More Repeat Customers" is useless as a BHI without some way for you to distinguish between **new and repeat**

customers. "Be The Most Popular Company" won't work as a BHI because there is no way for you to measure your company's popularity or compare it to others.

It is also important to define the BHIs and stay with the same definition from year to year. For a BHI of "Increase Sales", you need to address considerations like whether to measure by units sold or by dollar value of sales. Will returns be deducted from sales in the month of the sale or the month of the return? Will sales be recorded for the BHI at list price or at the actual sales price?

You also need to **set targets** for each BHI.

A company goal to be the employer of choice might include a BHI of "Turnover Rate". After the BHI has been defined as "the number of voluntary resignations and terminations for performance, divided by the total number of employees at the beginning of the period" and a way to measure it has been set up by collecting the information in a Human Resources Information System, the target has to be established.

"Reduce turnover by five percent per year" is a clear target that everyone will understand and be able to take **specific action** to accomplish.

Focus On The Essentials

Many things are measurable, but that does not make them key to your company success. In selecting BHIs, it is critical to limit them to those factors that are **essential** to you reaching your company goals.

If you set a goal "to be the most profitable company in our industry" you will have BHIs that **measure profit** and related fiscal measures. "Pre-tax Profit" and "Shareholder Value" will be among them.

However, a BHI of "Percent of Profit Contributed to Community Causes" probably will not be something you measure in relation to this goal.

It is also important to keep the number of BHIs small, since overwhelming people (yourself included!) with numbers and things to track is not going to get you anywhere.

It goes without saying, there's a reason they are called **Business HEALTH Indicators!!**

That is not to say that your company will have only three or four total BHIs. Rather there will be three or four BHIs for the overall company and then all the units within it will have three, four or five BHIs that support the overall company goals and can be **"rolled up"** into them.

Key Marketing BHIs

Now we've talked a lot about BHIs in general for your business, but what about your marketing efforts specifically?

While there is no "one size fits all" set of metrics that all businesses can apply to their marketing efforts, there are several BHIs that you should

track to ensure that you are getting the marketing results your business needs.

Here are some of the Marketing BHIs (just the name—not how it relates to your business; you have to figure that one out yourself) you should begin to track in your business (no particular order):

- **New leads per month** (overall & by specific segment effort) – The percentage rate at which your mass marketing drives new leads to your business (i.e. initial response rate).

- **Lead to qualified prospect conversion** – The percentage rate at which your leads convert to qualified prospects (i.e. they are identified as being a qualified prospect who wants/needs what you sell and are capable of making a buying decision).

- **Qualified prospect to client conversion** – The percentage rate at which your qualified prospects convert into buyers (customers).

- **Customer response levels** – Your ability to respond to inbound customer requests whether sales or support related.

- **Return / refund rates** – The average rate at which a customer requests a return, exchange or refund of a product or service purchased from you.

- **Cost per acquisition (CPA)** – The average cost of all marketing efforts divided by the number of new paying customers you acquire.

- **Overall marketing Return On Investment (ROI)** – Your overall return on investment of all marketing dollars per month, quarter and year.

- **Customer attrition** – The number of customers who cease doing business with you for any reason.

Of course you can add many more BHIs and get way more specific in the areas of your marketing efforts that **drive your business.**

Tracking & Testing My Marketing

It is important to track and test everything that you do as it relates to your marketing efforts. Even the slightest change in the headline of an advertisement can have **dramatic results** on the overall effectiveness of that ad.

Once you have developed a marketing system that works to provide you with positive ROI and is building your business, **constantly test** changes to that system in isolation— one change at a time so you know exactly what is affecting the results—in order to continually and gradually improve your efforts.

Understanding ROI

One of the biggest mistakes of new business owners is to incorrectly calculate the appropriate Return On Investment (ROI) for their marketing efforts. So here's a quick test to see how you do ...

If you spend $1000 on a marketing campaign and it generates $2000 in revenue, has this been a **successful marketing campaign?** Have you just made a cool $1000?

What if I told you that your typical business net profit was 20%? This would mean that 80% of all the revenue you generated was sucked up in your business costs, before you'd even begun to pay for the marketing campaign. On the $2000 in revenue this would actually leave you with $400, out of which you'd then have to cover the cost of the campaign at $1000. This leaves you with a $600 loss. Suddenly, it doesn't seem quite as successful, does it?

So, if you look to simply make more than $1000 from a $1000 investment then you're probably actually losing money when everything is considered.

In the example above, if your net profit for the business is 20% then whatever you spend on marketing needs to generate at least a 5x the return in order to actually start **generating a profit** overall for the business.

Here's why—$5000 in revenue at a 20% net profit is $1000 in profit. This would then pay for the costs of the marketing campaign. Anything you generate from this campaign after the $5000 revenue mark is reached can then start counting as profit for your company.

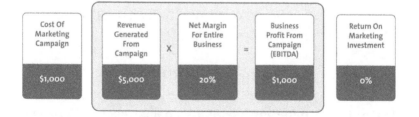

Download the FREE "Marketing Profit Calculator" at
www.MakeMyMarketingWorkBook.com.

Remember this when planning and tracking the return on your marketing! It's okay to get a lower return on your investment, so long as its part of your planned strategy. Otherwise, it's just a poor return!

Test Everything

Another one of the big mistakes business owners and their staff make, particularly in the marketing arena, is making permanent decisions based on emotion or **"gut feel"**.

Notice the word "permanent". Obviously you will have to rely on your experience and gut feeling initially, but the sooner you can move to making informed decisions based on actual results, the better.

For example, your gut may tell you that a particular headline will grab the attention of your target audience and draw them in to an advertisement, creating an **avalanche** of new leads. But someone else on your team may be equally sure that your headline will have the exact opposite effect, believing that their headline is the one that you should go forward with.

So who is right? Which headline should you proceed with?

The answer: **both!**

Test the two different headlines against each other—and against your control headline, if you have one that is already producing a positive ROI—and see which produces the better results.

If your headline wins in the only test that really matters (its ability to bring about a positive ROI), then it becomes your control headline and the others are discarded. The same is true for the other headline.

◀)) Insider Tip:

Don't let your ego get in the way of making the best decision for your business. If someone else on your team suggests a change that returns a better result in your testing, make it the control (the one you measure any new variations against) and celebrate the fact that you just improved the company profit—something that is a huge WIN for everyone involved.

What else can you test? An easier question to answer is what CAN'T you test? Anything and everything can—and should—be tested and measured when it comes to your marketing efforts. And every change, no matter how small it may seem to you, should be tested in isolation.

Why Track Changes In Isolation?

Let's say you have an advertisement that is performing reasonably well and is generating a positive ROI. This ad then becomes your "control"—the one you measure any new variations against from a purely performance perspective. That is, you determine what the ad is intended to do (increase leads, drive sales, etc) and **test the performance** of any changes against that criteria. If the change produces a better result, it then becomes the control against which future changes are measured.

If it does not produce a better result, it is removed from use.

But if you change multiple aspects of a campaign, you'll never know which element caused the change, regardless of whether it was positive or negative.

As a marketer—and if you're in business you're in marketing, whether you like it or not—then it's your job not only to get to the point of positive ROI on all your efforts, but also to **maximize your ROI** by continually refining your marketing message.

Test Changes In Small Doses!

We're not suggesting that you make changes and test them across the board. If your change backfires, you could seriously damage your company's reputation and profitability in the short and long term.

Instead, test your changes in small segments. Try that new headline in a regional paper before rolling it out nationally. Test different versions of your direct mail piece against your control version to small segments of your list until **you have a powerhouse** mailer that is proven to pull the numbers you need to be successful. Then, and only then, do you want to send it to the masses.

Testing changes is imperative to your **long term success!**

Let us be blunt. Failing to constantly assess, track and test improvements to your marketing activities is leaving money on the table. This is money your competitors will be more than happy to come by and pick up for you.

Setting A Marketing Budget

So, we've talked a lot about "doing stuff" throughout this program. As I'm sure most of you have noticed in life, "stuff" tends to cost money.

Now a lot of what we've talked about in the program actually doesn't cost **vast sums of money,** but it can still add up pretty quickly. Therefore, the question is, are you going to just spend money, or are you going to have a planned-out strategic marketing budget?

You may be sitting there saying, "I don't generate that much revenue—why do I need a marketing budget?" Or "I've never had a marketing budget before, why start now?"

Well ask yourself this—have you ever spoken to an advertising sales rep trying to sell you ad space? Sounds like it could be a good deal but you're not too sure if you can afford it?

What if you could have all your marketing expenses planned out for the year. Then, when reps call you can politely say, "sorry my budget is already set for this year. Call back in November when I'm planning for next year".

Now you don't have to worry about whether this is going to be the **latest greatest thing** for your business. You don't have to spend time working out if you can afford it. All you have to do is keep on executing on the plan you already have in place.

Or, if you have a little "wiggle room" you'll know that too and can proceed accordingly.

A planned out marketing budget also **holds you accountable** to actually spending the money on your business. Many business owners get stuck in the vicious trap of saying something like, "I'm going to spend $40,000 on marketing this year".

However, maybe the business doesn't perform as well as expected or there's another bill to be paid and guess what? Unless the marketing expenses have been planned out and committed to, the business owner doesn't spend the cash on marketing, and thus, the business suffers.

**No marketing =
no exposure =
no sales =
NO MONEY!**

Also, by having a marketing budget, you'll always know where you are in terms of your **marketing cash flow.** You won't suddenly get to the end of the year and go "Ooooops—we spent twice as much as we can actually afford on marketing this year". Or even worse, "I wish I had spent more. My business has really suffered because we didn't proactively spend enough".

We could write an entire book on how to create an effective marketing budget for the year. However, we're going to **keep it nice and simple** for you. So there are no excuses to not give it a go!

Exercise:

Create a simple and basic marketing budget.

Step 1: Note down your projected annual revenue for the next 12 months.

Step 2: Note the % of your annual revenue that you will spend on marketing. Somewhere between 10% – 25% is typical.

Step 3: Multiply your total revenue (step 1) by the percentage allocation (step 2). This will give you the budgeted amount of money to spend in total over the next 12 months.

Step 4: Unless your business generates revenue on a seasonal or other fluctuating basis, divide your total budget by 12 to get your monthly marketing budget. This will now show you how much you should spend on a monthly basis.

Step 5: Go back to the notes you've so far and look at all the ways you are going to deliver your marketing message. How many of these are actually going to cost something (i.e. business cards, direct mail pieces, yellow pages, Google ad words, etc)? List them all out and how much each will cost.

Step 6: Now, create a chart and list the actual amounts you need to spend, **in the months you're going to spend it.** Compare this to the monthly "budget" from step 4. Once you have done this and totaled up the spending you'll have the very basic essence of the budget complete.

Step 7: You may notice in this first draft that some months you're spending way too much and too little in others. Also, how are you doing on your total spend for the year? Too much, too little—interesting isn't it? Go through your budget month-by-month, item-by-item and ensure that everything balances so that you're not spending too much or too little.

Download the Marketing Budget worksheet at: www.MakeMyMarketingWorkBook.com.

◀))) **Insider Tip:**

You may find that planning out your marketing evenly across the year (even taking into account seasonal variances) doesn't really work for you. Maybe you have a big trade show in June that sucks up 30% of your marketing budget for the entire year. That's okay; rather than overspending in June and then under spending for the rest of the year, simply amend the monthly budget to reflect this big spend.

Now you have a great working model for a marketing budget that can help you **stay on track** with your marketing spend, and ensure you are committed to spending the appropriate amount.

Funnel My Marketing

Having a defined marketing funnel in which to apply everything you've learned up to this point is crucial if you want to have a highly productive (not to mention profitable!) marketing program.

The Marketing Funnel is exactly what it sounds like. It is very wide at one end and very narrow at the other. It illustrates the process by which leads are qualified into potential buyers and then transformed into actual customers.

It is a predetermined set of steps your prospects will take on their way to eventually **becoming your customer.** It begins with the first time they hear about your product, service or company, followed by a period of education and familiarization and finally ends when they make the decision to **purchase from you.** This process can be very quick or very long depending on your unique situation. If you have a high cost item, such as a car, yacht or home, the funnel process may take quite a bit longer than if you are selling a $20 toaster.

There are three primary phases of the funnel, where there is a vetting or narrowing of the field of prospects at each level. The further down the funnel, the narrower the field and the fewer the prospects. Even though there are fewer of them, the **value of each prospect** rises the further down the funnel they go since the more educated they become, the more valuable they are if they choose to stick around.

Stage One: Introduce

During the introduction phase of the funnel your prospects have heard about your company and are starting to **get to know you.** They have seen your advertisements, publicity or other marketing efforts and their interest has been aroused. You have now entered their awareness.

At this point, your prospect may visit your website or store to find out more about you. Or, they may begin conducting some other research about who you are and **what you are selling.** They may ask their friends and colleagues, or they may "Google" you to find out if anyone has published any experiences or opinions about your company.

Using the strategies you outlined in this program, your primary goal in this stage of the funnel is simply to introduce and generate interest in the target market(s).

Make My Marketing Work

Stage Two: Inform

Once their interest has been aroused and they are actively inquiring into your business, it is your job to **inform them.** Stylistically, how you inform your prospects will depend largely on your specific business model, but a primary trait of the inform stage is to educate your prospect as much possible.

There are two important things you want to accomplish in the "inform" stage of your funnel. They are:

1. **Prove your claims** – In your initial marketing message you made some claims as to what your offering can do for people who purchase it. That helped create some interest, but it is not the end of the story. You now need to prove that what you claimed is actually true.

   Proof of claim can be done by showing the successes of others who have already purchased from you in the form of testimonials or success stories. You can also prove your claims by showing laboratory test results, industry or media reviews, or by referring to 3rd-party assessments.

2. **Remove barriers to entry** – People are naturally skeptical, and who can blame them? We've all been burned in the past and this creates a natural reluctance for fear of being burned again. As the old saying goes, "Once bitten, twice shy".

   The onus of removing barriers to entry falls squarely on your lap and is a critical part of the "inform" stage of the marketing funnel.

Does your offering have:
- Technical limitations (skills or minimum system requirements)?
- Age, weight or height restrictions (like some roller coasters)?
- Health restrictions (as with some exercise programs)?
- High financial investment?
- High risk vs. low reward?

Being up front about the potential barriers to entry and finding ways to diffuse them is a necessary step at this point in the funnel process.

Things that can help reduce or eliminate barriers to entry for your prospects include:
- Offering a strong guarantee (risk reversal)
- Increase value with "value add" bonuses
- Offer payment terms
- Try before you buy

◀)) Insider Tip:

This is starting to sound a lot like SELLING..... Well, marketing and selling (sales) are joined at the hip and cannot be easily separated.

In fact, good marketing will almost always result in sales or a qualified lead for the majority of small businesses.

Stage Three: Integrate

This is the point at which you and your prospect agree to do business together, thereby integrating your interests and entering into a formal relationship with each other. They purchase; you provide.

But in order for them to purchase, you need to ask them for the sale.

That's important, so we're going to say it again: **You need to ask them for the sale!**

The number one reason most people don't get the sale is because they don't **ask for the sale.** They think that by generating interest and informing their prospects, the integration step will naturally and automatically happen.

Sometimes it does, if the buyer is already motivated or if you sell a "fast moving consumer good" (FMCG) like milk. More often than not though, it's up to you to **ask for the sale.** You do that by giving them a strong call to action and a compelling reason to act now.

1. **Create "buy now" urgency** – What is going to get your prospect to make a buying decision today, right now? Not tomorrow, not after they "think about it"—NOW!

   There are lots of tactics used to create this kind of urgency, but they all come down to one primary strategy: Scarcity.

Scarcity can be used in many different ways in order to get the desired effect. Some to consider are:

- Limitation (Quantity) – The first 10 people to act save!
- Limitation (Time) – Price increases in one week. Buy now!
- Limitation (Benefits) – Don't suffer that ugly red rash for even one more week. Get your miracle cream today!

◄)) Insider Tip:

This is starting to sound a lot like SELLING ... well; marketing and selling (sales) are joined at the hip and cannot be easily separated.

In fact, good marketing will almost always result in sales or a qualified lead for the majority of small businesses.

 ## Exercise:

List out a several specific "buy now" tactics that you can use to create urgency for your product or service.

Download the Customer Integration worksheet at www.MakeMyMarketingWorkBook.com.

2. **Have a strong "call to action"** – Even with a heightened sense of urgency and limitation, many

prospects will not initiate the buying process of their own volition. They need to be called to action.

A call to action could be to clip out and mail in a coupon, visit your website, call a toll free number or come to your store. When combined with a powerful limiter, your specific call to action will motivate prospects to become buyers and exit your front-end funnel (your marketing efforts), preparing them for your back-end funnel (your on-going sales efforts).

 Exercise:

List out several different "calls to action" that you can use to motivate potential customers to take immediate action.

Download the Customer Integration worksheet at www.MakeMyMarketingWorkBook.com.

Think about this from a practical perspective for a moment and you'll see just why the funnel analogy makes so much sense.

When you send out a mass media advertisement, such as a newspaper advertisement, you are perhaps reaching the awareness of the entire readership which might be 100,000 people. Does it make sense to expect that every single one of those people who see your ad will respond to it? Of course not.

Not every person will need what you're selling. So there is an automatic narrowing of people who are interested in your advertisement. Those who are your target market move in slightly while the rest flip out of the funnel.

Then a certain percentage of those people who are interested will begin to investigate your company, product or service, etc., to find out if it truly is a **match for them.** They will respond (either favorably or unfavorably) to things like price, benefits and return policy, as well as the intangible things we talked about earlier, such as the experience they have when visiting your store or website, the level of service they receive, etc.

The sum total of their response will either cause them to jump out of your funnel or they will continue to **inquire and investigate,** moving deeper into it.

Finally, prospects will be presented with a buying question. They will either say "Yes" or they will say "No". Unless you are willing to leave money on the table, the conversation should NOT end there!

If the customer says yes, and decides to buy, you now have an opportunity to **cross sell or up sell them.** If they say no, then you can down sell them on something else, particularly if the reason for not buying was related to price.

Cross Selling

Cross selling (also known as Add-On Selling) occurs when a customer has already made a purchasing decision and the sales person (or automated process, if the sale is occurring online) generates an example of additional products or services that would compliment the initial purchase.

"Would you like fries with that?" is a classic cross sell example, as is the cross selling system popularized by Amazon.com that suggestively informs you that "people who bought X also bought Y".

Things like extra vacuum bags for a new vacuum cleaner, an extended warranty for that new MP3 player or 12 months of basic maintenance for a new car would be considered cross selling.

Anything that enhances or compliments the product or service they have already decided to purchase is considered cross selling. More examples would be leather seating and air conditioning plus that all important new car undercoating, or a bike helmet and roadside tire repair kit.

Up Selling

Up selling occurs when you let your customer know about the other vacuum you sell that is more expensive, but which has better suction and more tools for those hard to reach places; or, **informing them** of the new video MP3 player that is also a phone, scheduler and calculator instead of the basic model they were looking at initially.

Up selling is getting someone out of the 2-door hatchback and into the more expensive sport utility vehicle; **upgrading** from an economy seat to first class; or upgrading from a condo to a fully detached home.

Down Selling

This is used as a strategy to **retain a customer** who has said no in the initial buying conversation, particularly when the reason they declined was based on price.

In these cases, a lesser version of the product or service may be offered, with less "value added" bonuses, at a reduced price that they can more easily afford.

Selling a used car instead of a new car, a broom instead of a vacuum, or making any of the moves in the up selling section in the opposite direction would all be examples of down selling.

The benefit to down selling is that by completing a sale with the prospect, thereby turning them into a customer, you give yourself the opportunity to **prove the value** of your product or service. This opens the door to future business with them.

Too often companies neglect to use the down sell approach when they hear a no after asking for the sale, essentially leaving money on the table. Without a down selling attempt, the prospect is never given the opportunity to be remarketed to in the future.

The Bottom Of The Funnel

Congratulations! You have, at least in theory, successfully converted a prospect into a customer and made a sale.

What you do next could determine whether the relationship fizzles out or grows. Are you going to ignore your new customer and leave them to their own devices to figure out the best way to use your product? Or are you going to **keep the dialog going,** offering continuing education and information, and being a valuable resource?

Keep communicating with your client in a useful and value-added way (i.e. latest special offers, consumer reports, etc), and you stand a much better chance of attracting their future business.

Also, reviewing each phase of your marketing funnel and how it is performing will help you stay on top of the game when it comes to maximizing your results.

As you've learned, what you measure improves. So keep a close eye on what is working and what isn't. Make a habit to sit down monthly with your coach or mentor (if you don't have one, GET ONE!) and review the funnel process you have in place: **Identify challenges**; brainstorm new ideas for each; and then get to work implementing them. Track everything you do so that you are always aware of what is working and what isn't.

◀)) Insider Tip:

Reviewing your results on a monthly basis with a mentor, advisor or coach has proven to be CRITICAL for many business owners. As the owner of the business, it's often difficult (and even inappropriate) to turn to others within the business for accountability, feedback and advice. It's also a difficult task to effectively do yourself as you're so close to the business. So having someone external to help you can really help you see clearly and get huge results!

Remember, the marketplace is constantly changing and what works today may be outdated tomorrow. Having **monthly reviews** of your funnel process will allow you to identify changes that are occurring or about to occur within the marketplace and adapting early will keep you in the competitive arena.

TIME OUT!
(Pause, Breath, Review)

You've now got a solid grasp of the key marketing metrics (BHIs) that you must track in your business in order to be successful.

You've looked at the importance of accurately tracking your ROI. Also, you understand why testing changes to your marketing in isolation is imperative to positively impacting your ROI over the long term.

You looked at the three primary levels of a front-end marketing funnel; how to squeeze your prospects down the funnel; and developed up sell, down sell and cross sell programs.

SECTION 5 :: Pulling It All Together!

> ### In This Section You Will:
>
> ✓ Learn THE most important aspect of creating a successful strategic marketing program.
> ✓ Take ACTION to ensure your success!

You now have the ability to look at your marketing efforts from a **strategic perspective** and effectively evaluate which tactics will be most appropriate (and profitable) for your business!

With your new knowledge, we're sure that you have come up with tons of new ideas about how to more effectively market your business.

You may think that, as you read these final pages, everything is complete and your job is almost finished...

But The Journey Has Just Begun!

Our experience working with countless business owners just like you has shown that having knowledge is one thing—applying it is something else altogether!

Hopefully you've downloaded all the worksheets from www.MakeMyMarketingWorkBook.com and have used them as you read each section of this book.

If you have, then you already have a taste of the power of implementation, the results that come with focused, strategic action.

You may find yourself with an amazing amount of ideas floating around and lots of scribbled notes but no clear written plan to execute them.

Even if you do have some kind of plan, the statistics are still stacked against you and the likelihood that you'll get **maximum results** from the plan without the necessary habits and support systems in place is very low.

But don't feel bad about that, because you're in the same situation as just about everyone else out there. The big difference is that you are aware of this critical need and are in a unique position to do something about it.

The real question is: **What Action Are You Going To Take?**

If you want to beat the statistics that are currently stacked against you, there's another critical step you must take.

This next step—the golden key to unlocking your potential and the way to move into the top 1% of business owners— is to recognize that true marketing POWER in any business lies not in having knowledge, but in taking **ACTION** with that knowledge to get real results!

With that in mind it's now critical to your future success that you compile all your notes into a formal written "strategic marketing plan" that clearly outlines all your "tactical marketing actions" and helps you create some powerful "marketing habits" that will ensure you take consistent action in the right areas, over the long term.

To help you assess your current knowledge level and determine the best course of action to take next, we have prepared a simple, yet powerful self assessment—perhaps the most important exercise of the whole book for you to complete!

Be honest with yourself when rating your current knowledge—give yourself credit where it is due and acknowledge those areas where you may still need additional help.

 ## Exercise:

Read the questions below and rate yourself from 1 to 10. A score of "1" is the lowest and a "10" means "you rock".

1. I have a detailed, written marketing plan.

| 1 | 2 | 3 | 4 | 5 | 6 | 7 | 8 | 9 | 10 |

2. My marketing efforts produce measurable results.

| 1 | 2 | 3 | 4 | 5 | 6 | 7 | 8 | 9 | 10 |

3. My marketing messages, style of presentation and frequency of interaction are consistent with my core values and budget.

| 1 | 2 | 3 | 4 | 5 | 6 | 7 | 8 | 9 | 10 |

4. My marketing is systematized, recurring and seemingly effortless.

| 1 | 2 | 3 | 4 | 5 | 6 | 7 | 8 | 9 | 10 |

5. I know what motivates my customers to want to do business with me over my competition.

| 1 | 2 | 3 | 4 | 5 | 6 | 7 | 8 | 9 | 10 |

6. I have a clear vision of where I want to take my business.

| 1 | 2 | 3 | 4 | 5 | 6 | 7 | 8 | 9 | 10 |

7. I fully understand and leverage the F.A.B. of my products/services.

| 1 | 2 | 3 | 4 | 5 | 6 | 7 | 8 | 9 | 10 |

8. My marketing program reflects my company culture.

| 1 | 2 | 3 | 4 | 5 | 6 | 7 | 8 | 9 | 10 |

9. I understand where my customers come from.

| 1 | 2 | 3 | 4 | 5 | 6 | 7 | 8 | 9 | 10 |

10. I have a USP that clearly conveys my "big promise".

| 1 | 2 | 3 | 4 | 5 | 6 | 7 | 8 | 9 | 10 |

Now, total up all the scores from your answers and write it down: _____

How did you do? What was your score? Let's have a look at what it means ...

0 – 27: Unfortunately, your Marketing IQ (and therefore chance for success) is very low. That doesn't mean you have a bad business idea—it just means that you need to strengthen your marketing knowledge, habits and skills— As Soon As Possible!

If you didn't complete the exercises in this book, go back to the beginning and re-read it and be sure to do them—they are there for a reason!

If you did the exercises and still scored low, consider investing in additional training materials, books and coaching to help you gain additional knowledge, create a plan and develop both the habits and skills to be successful.

28 – 84: You rank among the average when it comes to strategic marketing, but there is still room for improvement. Having a series of plans that govern your monthly goals as well as your weekly and daily activities will help ensure that you implement the knowledge that you've already developed. A marketing & business coach can help keep you focused and on-track, while providing an objective view of your marketing message, target market and tactical plan.

85 – 100: Your marketing foundation is set and will serve you well as you continue to build your business. The next phase of your marketing education is the growth phase, during which you'll incrementally improve specific areas of your marketing, sales and business systems to create a compounding effect on your profits (just like compound interest does). A coach and marketing mentor can help you discover the hidden profit potential that lies within your existing systems with specific ideas about how to unlock it and add it directly to your bottom line!

So, what's next?

Where do you need to go from here?

How can you take all this information and actually create a detailed strategic marketing plan that lists out all your tactics and helps you create a habit around implementation?

How do you begin to **MAKE MORE MONEY** with everything you know about strategic marketing?

While you may be able to pull everything together successfully yourself given the marketing education you've gained in this book the chances are pretty slim. Which is why many people have worked with a Make My Marketing Work Coach to help them get things done right—done now—and done first time!

Quite literally, the very survival of your business could rest on what action you take now.

You could …

Do Nothing :: Treat the book as finished and you'll undoubtedly improve your results based on what you've learned. But will it be enough to really survive and even better, thrive?

Take Action :: To help you "TAKE ACTION" we've arranged a private, one-on-one (and 100% free) marketing strategy session to help you get the maximum result from this book and the marketing plan you've just created.

We want to see you increase your level of success!

ACTION BONUS

ABOUT THE AUTHORS

PAUL KEETCH

A lifelong entrepreneur, Paul started his first business at the age of 13, selling personalized gifts, then vacuums at 16, both door-to-door and has never looked back. He has owned several successful businesses including Brokenfeet Web Design and Atlas Avenue Artist Management.

His professional career has focused primarily on helping fast-moving, entrepreneurial technology- and knowledge-based companies focus their vision, develop strategic goals and the tactical plans to achieve them.

Paul has had the very good fortune to work with some of the world's thought leaders, including Dr. Deepak Chopra, Dr. Brian Greene and Dr. David Suzuki, among countless others.

Most recently, Paul has used his marketing expertise in a consulting role for high-level entrepreneurs including Mark Victor Hansen (co-creator, Chicken Soup for the Soul), Christine Comaford (author, Rules For Renegades) and Libby Gill (the branding brain behind Dr. Phil).

Paul is committed to helping ordinary businesses achieve extraordinary results.

Visit Paul at:
www.PaulKeetch.com

ALEX READ

As a seasoned entrepreneur, and recipient of the Business In Vancouver "40 Under 40" award, Alex owns several successful businesses across North America. These include a number of hyper-growth franchises with 1-800-GOT-JUNK?, and the popular Millionaire Prep School.

Alex brings to everything a wealth of international business and leadership experience having worked in several countries around the world. These include such places as the UK, Australia, New Zealand, Bahrain and Canada. Previously in his career he has worked in a variety of senior leadership roles for companies such as American Express and 1-800-GOT-JUNK?.

His primary career focus has been in Marketing and Operations, especially in fast growing privately held companies. During this time Alex has developed a passion for increasing organizational effectiveness through clear and transparent leadership. With an in-depth understanding of entrepreneurial hyper-growth enterprise, Alex is able to create calm out of chaos and lead an organization to new plateaus of success.

Alex holds an honors degree in Marketing and is an avid volunteer working on many youth development projects.

Visit Alex at:
www.AskAlexRead.com

BUY A SHARE OF THE FUTURE IN YOUR COMMUNITY

These certificates make great holiday, graduation and birthday gifts that can be personalized with the recipient's name. The cost of one S.H.A.R.E. or one square foot is $54.17. The personalized certificate is suitable for framing and will state the number of shares purchased and the amount of each share, as well as the recipient's name. The home that you participate in "building" will last for many years and will continue to grow in value.

Here is a sample SHARE certificate:

YES, I WOULD LIKE TO HELP!

I support the work that Habitat for Humanity does and I want to be part of the excitement! As a donor, I will receive periodic updates on your construction activities but, more importantly, I know my gift will help a family in our community realize the dream of homeownership. **I would like to SHARE in your efforts against substandard housing in my community!** *(Please print below)*

PLEASE SEND ME _____ SHARES at $54.17 EACH = $ $_____

In Honor Of: _____

Occasion: (Circle One)   HOLIDAY   BIRTHDAY   ANNIVERSARY

      OTHER: _____

Address of Recipient: _____

Gift From: _____ *Donor Address:* _____

Donor Email: _____

I AM ENCLOSING A CHECK FOR $ $_____ PAYABLE TO HABITAT FOR HUMANITY <u>OR</u> PLEASE CHARGE MY VISA OR MASTERCARD *(CIRCLE ONE)*

Card Number _____ Expiration Date: _____

Name as it appears on Credit Card _____ Charge Amount $ _____

Signature _____

Billing Address _____

Telephone # Day _____ Eve _____

PLEASE NOTE: Your contribution is tax-deductible to the fullest extent allowed by law.
Habitat for Humanity • P.O. Box 1443 • Newport News, VA 23601 • 757-596-5553
www.HelpHabitatforHumanity.org